50 MARTIAL ARTS
MYTHS

*You've seen the movies.
You've heard the tales.
Now, for the first time ever,
a new book unlocking the truth to...*

50 MARTIAL ARTS MYTHS

SULAIMAN SHARIF

NEW MEDIA ENTERTAINMENT LTD
New York, New York

© copyright 2009 New Media Entertainment, Ltd.

Copyrighted material. All rights reserved. No reproduction, reselling, reprinting, or republishing, in whole or in part, is permitted.

There is no warranty as to the accuracy of the material contained herein and it may not be relied upon for any purpose.

ISBN: 9780967754628

Library of Congress Control Number: 2009942484

Cover image: ninja: istock©bubbalove; blood splatter: istock©sbayram.
Pages: istock©123foto, page 18; istock©AndreyUshakov, page 102; istock©arsenik, page 2, 150; istock©Banannaanna, page 42; istock©Berryspun, 126; istock©Bluberries, 146; istock©Cimmerian, page viii; istock©cglade, page 86; istock©cynoclub, 134; istock©DanBrandenburg, page 6; istock©dial-a-view, page 78; istock©drxy, 154; istock©DYashkin, page 30; istock©emyerson, page 26; istock©ericcote, page 198; istock©felixmizioznikov, page 178; istock©fotografstockholm, page 98; istock©geotrac, page 38; istock©Gerville, page 22, 34, 58, 66, 70, 90, 94, 106, 110, 114, 118, 138, 142, 158, 162, 170, 182, 190, 194, 202; istock©huaxiadragon, 130; istock©KingWu, page 4, 10, 74; istock©Ljupco, page 174; istock©Malven, page 186; istock©Medini, page 55; istock©pascalgenest, page 166; istock©paparazzit, page 50; istock©Portugal2004, page 46; istock©proxyminder, page 122; istock©Roob, pages ii–iii; istock©vfoto, page 62; istock©YouraPechkin, page 14, 82.

Book design by DesignForBooks.com

CONTENTS

Introduction		1
1	The Shaolin Monastery is the Origin of All Martial Arts	5
2	If You Really Want to Learn Martial Arts, Today's Shaolin Temple is Still the Best Place to Go	11
3	Judo and Karate are Traditional Martial Arts	15
4	The West Has No Martial Arts Tradition of Its Own	19
5	Martial Arts are Out of Date	23
6	There's No Such Thing as Bad Martial Arts	27
7	Martial Arts is All About Winning Fights	31
8	Martial Arts is All About Spirituality	35
9	Martial Arts Increases Aggressiveness in Its Students	39
10	Martial Arts is a Sport and Has Nothing to Do with Real Fighting	43
11	True Martial Arts is Always Unarmed	47
12	One Martial Arts Form Is Better Than All the Others	51
13	One Fighter Is Better Than All the Others	55
14	Kung Fu is the Most Popular Martial Art	59
15	Tai Chi is Not a Martial Art	63
16	If a Martial Arts Style was Really Effective, It Would Form a Part of Military Training	67

17	Girls Can't and Shouldn't Do Martial Arts	71
18	Martial Arts is Only for the Young	75
19	Size and Strength are Irrelevant in Martial Arts	79
20	To Do Martial Arts, You Have to Enjoy Physical Combat	83
21	To Develop the Strength for Martial Arts, You Have to Work Out and Consume Vast Quantities of Protein	87
22	Martial Arts Requires All Sorts of Bizarre and Expensive Equipment	91
23	Some Martial Arts Moves are So Dangerous That No Style Will Teach Them	95
24	To Fight Effectively, You Have to Channel Your Qi	99
25	Breaking Bricks is a Sign of Advanced Martial Arts Skill	103
26	Some Fighting Techniques are Unstoppable	107
27	Martial Arts Training is Dangerous	111
28	When Fighting an Attacker Armed with a Knife, You Can Always Stay Safe and Disarm Him Quickly	115
29	It's Possible to Train Without Sparring	119
30	If You're Good at Sparring, You're Ready for Fighting	123
31	Belts and Dans are Important Measurements of Martial Skill	127
32	Northern Kung Fu Kicks, Southern Kung Fu Punches	131
33	Aikido is a "Peaceful" Martial Art that Rejects the Use of Weapons	135
34	Mixed Martial Arts is a Modern Invention that Prioritizes Bloodshed Over Skill	139
35	Practiced Martial Artists Can Defend Themselves Against an Attacker Armed with a Firearm	143

36	Top Martial Artists Have to Register Their Hands as Weapons	147
37	Martial Artists Compete in Secret Death Matches	151
38	It Takes Years of Martial Arts Training Before You're Ready to Defend Yourself.	155
39	Anyone Can Set Themselves Up as a Martial Arts Instructor	159
40	Martial Arts Practitioners Have to Be at the Peak of Physical Fitness	163
41	Studying Martial Arts Means Doing All Sorts of Painful and Difficult Exercises	167
42	All Martial Arts are the Same	171
43	It's Enough to Learn How to Fight Standing Up	175
44	A Kick to the Groin is the Only Martial Arts Move You Need to Know	179
45	There's Nothing Artistic About Martial Arts	183
46	Martial Arts is the Same as Self-Defense	187
47	Qi Can't Really Turn You into a Better Martial Artist	191
48	A Trained Martial Artist Can Withstand Crippling Blows	195
49	Martial Artists Have to Be Subservient to Their Instructors	199
50	A True Martial Artist Will Never Reveal His Secrets	203

Conclusion	207
About the Author	209
Index	211

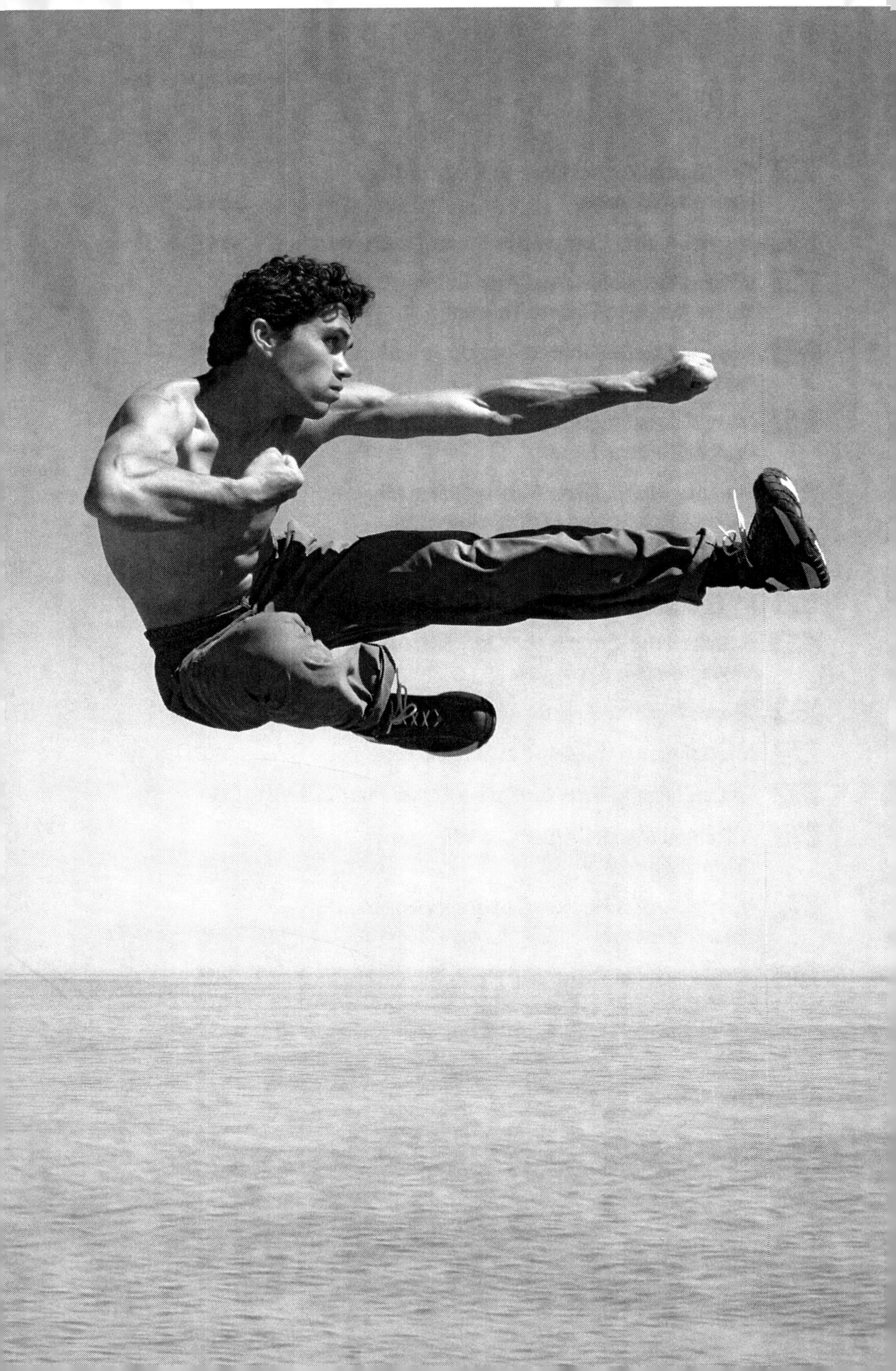

INTRODUCTION

Part of the appeal of martial arts is the stories: the kung fu films, the Jin Yong novels, the images of high-kicking Shaolin monks spinning through the air and using the mystical power of qi to dispatch teams of pajama-wearing bad guys. The myths that surround martial arts are as much a part of their attraction as the skills they provide to beat off muggers and defend loved ones.

But those stories can bring challenges too. The sight of lines of students repeating moves, bowing to teachers and training in the kind of controlled conditions that real fights never bring can lead many to believe that martial arts has nothing to do with self-defense. The shouts and the violence can put off parents concerned that that studying martial arts will turn their children into aggressive thugs. And the legends that have stuck to martial arts can cause some people to believe that the world's best fighters are those who survive secret death matches, who can kill with a single finger press and who can break a pile of bricks with a single forehead smash.

In fact, while martial arts and self-defense are different disciplines, they overlap in important and revealing ways. While martial arts is about the correct use of force, research has found that disciplined training actually reduces aggression. And while death matches, killing touches and brick breaking all make for dramatic tales, the truth is that gladiators went out with the Romans, pressure points are well-known and breaking bricks is

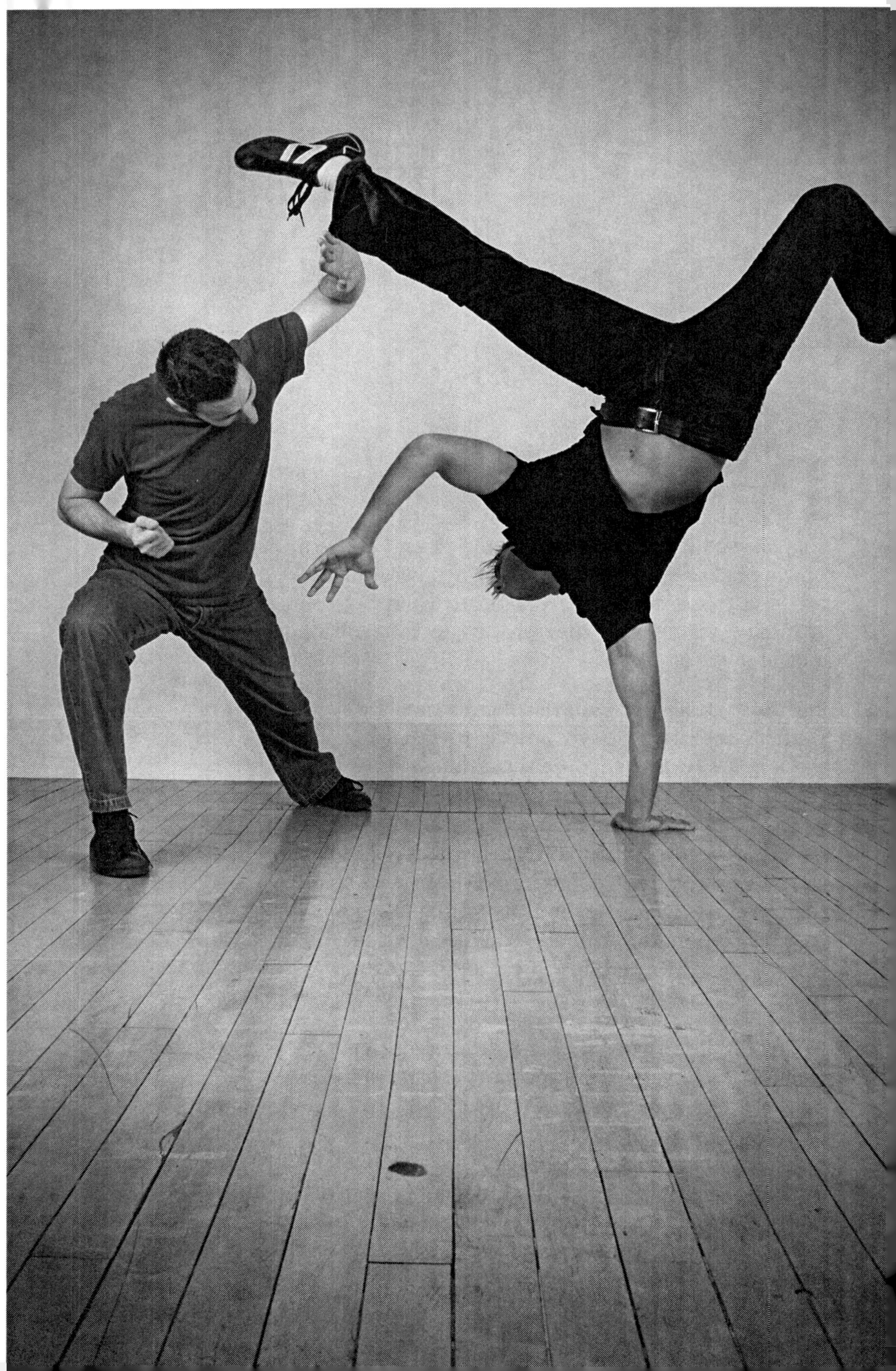

all about technique and training, and is not a sign of great martial arts skill.

With hundreds of different forms that range from Brittany to Brazil and from Mongolia to Africa, and with histories that stretch into antiquity, it's no surprise that the world's martial arts forms have picked up a romantic story or two. In this book, we're going to strip away some of the tallest tales told about martial arts to reveal the truth about combat training.

You'll still be left with a love of martial arts, a deep respect for its history and traditions, and an enthusiasm for its ability to provide discipline, focus, strength and skill. But you'll be better informed and possess a greater understanding of the real story of martial arts.

Shaolin temple main entrance, which where the Shaolin kung Fu were originated, Henan province, China.

MYTH 1

THE SHAOLIN MONASTERY IS THE ORIGIN OF ALL MARTIAL ARTS

Back in the days of the Wild West, there was only one fist-fighter the bad guys really feared. Kwai Chang Caine was a hard-punching half-American, half-Chinese orphan with a weakness for spiritualism and hands that were more dangerous than a gunslinger's holster. But Caine, a character played by David Carradine in the 1970's television series *Kung Fu*, wasn't just some bruiser who knew how to defend himself. He had grown up in the Shaolin monastery where he was trained by a Shaolin kung fu master—the ultimate source of all martial knowledge

There was a reason the show's producers chose Shaolin as the place where Caine was trained. For those who aren't familiar with the full range and variety of martial arts, it can appear that fighting skills have one central origin: a temple in China's Henan province where Buddhist monks copied the actions of birds and animals to produce a unique form of fighting from which all others developed. Some methods have enhanced the Shaolin style; others might have misinterpreted it, producing weaker versions that are no closer to the real thing than the last Chinese whisper is to the original message. But all forms of hand-to-hand fighting, it appears, owe their origins to Shaolin.

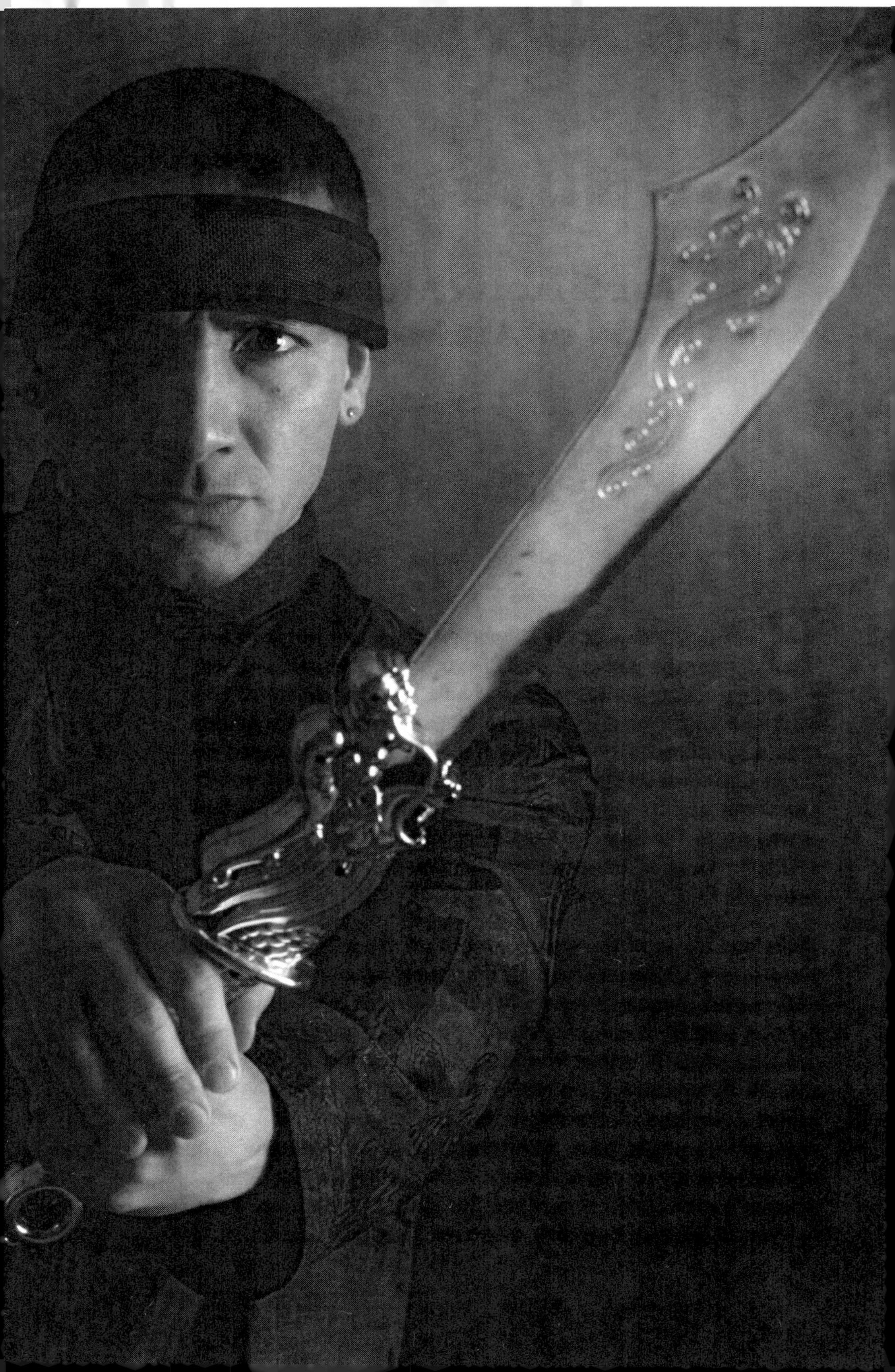

The truth though is very different. While the history and development of martial arts has certainly been heavily influenced by the fighting monks of the Shaolin temple—at least in the way martial arts are shown in movies, if not in their actual fighting forms—Shaolin is just one of many places where martial arts have been practiced.

And it certainly wasn't the first.

Even in China, martial arts have been around long before the foundation of the Shaolin temple in the fifth century. The *Spring and Autumn Annals*, a historical document dating from the eighth to the fifth centuries BC, mention "hard" and "soft" forms of martial arts. Other documents dating to the Han dynasty (206 BC–220 AD) refer to differences between sports wrestling and unarmed combat, for which manuals were available even then.

Nor was martial arts training restricted to China, even at this time. Pankration, a sport practiced at the Greek Olympics in 648 BC, combined wrestling and boxing to produce a complete system that included kicks, locks, throws and even chokes. A tournament might have looked a little like a modern mixed martial arts meet—except that pankration fighters fought naked, something that mixed martial artists tend to avoid.

In India too, the *Akananuru* and *Purananuru*, two poetry collections dating from around the first century AD and the second century BC describe a martial arts system using spears, swords, shields, bows and silambam, a kind of staff.

And the techniques used and taught by Roman gladiators and legionnaires might be considered a form of martial arts training too, even if they weren't spread widely, had little influence and are no longer practiced today.

In truth then, while Shaolin martial arts are certainly important, they're not the origin of training in armed and unarmed combat. Martial arts began in different places and at different times, in response to certain conditions—such as the attitude of local religions or the violence of the surrounding environment. Each form developed in its own way, influenced by local changes, by talented teachers who discovered ways to improve the technique or by meeting with other forms that inspired new moves altogether.

So how then did one temple in one country come to be seen as the model for all martial arts and the source of knowledge for hand-to-hand combat?

Much of the reason lies in Shaolin's history. The temple was founded on the slopes of Mount Song, one of the five holy peaks to which Chinese royals were supposed to pay homage. Located just 35 kilometers from Luoyang, an imperial capital, it was also easy to reach and was therefore given plenty of gifts from emperors keen to show their spiritual side.

The temple's links to royalty didn't stop with a fortunate location though. The first evidence that the monks took part in combat dates to the early seventh century, when they joined a campaign against bandits. In 621, Shaolin monks helped Li Shimin seize the imperial throne. As a reward, one of the monks was appointed General-in-Chief of the imperial army.

However, it's not until a thousand years later—during a time of banditry, violence and a weak imperial military—that we first see evidence that Shaolin monks actually engaged in a unique form of combat training. Texts dating to the seventeenth century describe Shaolin monks practicing spear-fighting, unarmed combat and, most importantly, fighting with a staff. That last technique might have been influenced by the fighting technique used by the Monkey King in *Journey to the West*, a hugely popular book that predates by two centuries the first known use of Shaolin skills.

It was also around this time that we begin to see the spread of the Shaolin myths. When the monks were called on to support the military in its campaigns against pirates, Friar Tianyuan, a Shaolin monk, was placed in charge of the monastic troops. Monks from Hangzhou challenged his command by picking eight champions to face him in combat. Tianyuan spotted them climbing towards his terrace and beat them off. When they attacked again with swords, Tianyuan used a door-bar to defeat and disarm them single-handedly, winning their respect and their obedience.

And that perhaps is the greatest evidence that Shaolin is not the source of all martial arts. The temple specialized not in animal forms but in fighting with a staff, a method rarely used today outside the ritualized sport of kendo. It is however a rich source of martial arts stories.

Shaoling Temple, Henan province, China.

MYTH 2

If You Really Want to Learn Martial Arts, Today's Shaolin Temple is Still the Best Place to Go

The Shaolin Temple might not be where martial arts started but it's certainly a center of martial arts now. Each year around 1.5 million people visit the temple, which was completely renovated in 2004 and now covers an area of around 20 square kilometers. Led by the first monk with an MBA, the temple is now as much a business as a cultural and religious center. It puts on performances, sells entrance tickets and memorabilia, and has licensed its name to video games, musicals and theatre performances. By the end of 2004 alone, the temple's performers had demonstrated their moves more than 10,000 times in more than 60 countries. An opera entitled *Shaolin in the Wind*, co-sponsored with the Zhengzhou Song and Dance Theatre, is said to have earned over $8 million, and in 2006, the temple teamed up with Shenzhen Satellite TV Station to create a reality show called the "Global Chinese Kung Fu Star TV Competition." You can think of it as an American Idol in which the judges fear the contestants.

The Shaolin Temple is clearly a great place to go if you're looking for martial arts entertainment. But is it a good place to go if you want to become a martial arts master?

Many people clearly think so. More than 30,000 come each year to study at the many martial arts schools scattered around the region. Some of those students come from abroad, staying for periods that range from a month to several years, before returning home with what they hope will be knowledge of true Shaolin martial arts.

The Shaolin Culture Training School in Zhengzhou, for example, offers classes in basic Shaolin kung fu, five step quan, luohan quan, seven star quan lian and a whole host of other techniques, as well as fighting with eighteen traditional weapons such as the tai chi sword. The school also offers Chinese language classes and lessons on martial arts theory, Buddhism and Taoism.

The Wudang Daoist Traditional Internal Kung Fu Academy also turns foreigners into hard-punching martial arts experts. Its courses include tai chi, xing yi, ba gua, qi gong and others under the leadership of Daoist priest Master Yuan Xiu Gang. Students can choose to study for periods from one month to a year.

Some students will clearly get a great deal out of these courses. If they're attracted to the kind of internal martial arts systems that Shaolin schools tend to teach, then they'll learn, advance and improve their skills. They won't become martial arts masters—that takes years of training and can't be crammed even into one academic year under a Master Yuan—but they should benefit from their time at one of the Shaolin schools.

But that doesn't mean it's necessary. Nor is it something that every martial arts student should do and it won't provide an education they couldn't have picked up with an equally good dojo at a local school.

That's because when you really want to learn martial arts, it doesn't matter where you go. It matters what you learn and who you choose to learn it from.

The first question to answer when you're looking for the right place to learn martial arts then isn't "Which is the most famous place connected to martial arts?" but "What kind of martial arts do I want to learn?" Although many of the different martial arts schools are connected, they all offer different skills and different benefits. Some are more defensive than others. They all require different training techniques, and they all appeal to different people in different ways. More important than where you're going to learn your martial arts is what sort of martial arts suit you best.

That's a question that only you can answer by looking at the different types of schools available in your area, reading about the techniques on offer and visiting them to talk to the trainers and watch the fighters in action.

But the second question is who you want to learn from and that's no less important.

Just because a martial arts teacher shares his knowledge in the shadow of Mount Song, doesn't mean that he's the most knowledgeable person on his type of fighting skill or the best person to share that knowledge with you.

As you visit a range of different martial arts schools—as you should—you'll find that martial arts teachers might all be skilled but they also come with different manners, approaches and styles. Some will demand absolute discipline and attempt to correct their students by shouting or yelling. Others will take a milder approach, motivating their students with compliments and praise.

The style and personality of the teacher count as much as the content of the classes themselves. Again, these can only be assessed by visiting the classes and talking to students there. Few martial arts trainers will object to you doing either of those.

When you're looking to learn one particular type of martial arts then, the Shaolin temple area might be a good place to go. Students who have studied there recently have reported that they've learned a great deal and benefitted hugely from the experience.

But the best place to study martial arts is never an ancient temple, a modern site with a good brand name or a school in the middle of nowhere. It's a place with the kind of martial arts that you want to study, taught by a teacher who inspires you and helps you to learn and grow.

That can be found anywhere, even half a world away from Shaolin.

MYTH **3**

JUDO AND KARATE ARE TRADITIONAL MARTIAL ARTS

When many people begin to consider taking up a martial art, they look for a technique that has a strong foundation. They want to learn fighting methods that have been tested over the years and found to be effective. And they want to belong to a fighting school that has a history, a culture and even a spirituality all of its own. Newer approaches such as mixed martial Arts or Israeli krav maga might have something to offer but they're nothing in comparison to the centuries-old methods and traditions of Shaolin kung fu, ba gua or many of the ancient Indian fighting styles.

And of judo and karate too. Both Japanese fighting techniques, judo's throws and grapples, and karate's powerful chops and kicks are as much a part of the image of martial arts as Shaolin's animal shapes and fighting monks. But are they really traditional martial arts—and how much does it matter?

Judo can be traced back to its founder, Japanese educator, Jigoro Kano. Born in 1860, Kano was a small and weak child who turned to jujitsu—a fighting technique first used by the Samurai—to protect himself. Jujitsu recognized the difficulty of striking against an armored opponent and attempted to use an attacker's momentum against him with throws, pins and grapples. Kano was an enthusiastic student who went on to study with some of the school's leading masters, noting the different emphases his teachers placed on practice and throwing techniques. It wasn't long before he was creating moves of his own, such as the "shoulder-wheel," a way of lifting opponents onto the shoulder, and the "floating hip" throw. At the age of 22, he began teaching in a Buddhist temple in Kamakura, a move now regarded as the founding of judo.

Kano's aim was to unite jujitsu's various techniques around a principle of maximum efficiency. Moves that relied on strength were replaced with moves that relied on the attacker's momentum or which made use of leverage. The result was a complete system that has gone on to become an Olympic sport.

Karate, on the other hand, failed to receive the two-thirds majority vote to join the Olympics. The practice began as a fighting system on the Ryukyu islands, now part of Japan, and originally consisted of a number of different styles, all influenced by fighting techniques from China. In fact, that influence can be seen in the original Kanji used in the technique's name: "karate" was originally written with characters that meant "Chinese hand." This was later changed to a phrase that meant "Empty hand" to emphasize karate's Japanese developments—and because as Japan went to war with China, it was unlikely that a fighting style with a Chinese name would win too many Japanese converts.

In fact, Funakoshi, the founder of shotokan karate, not only changed the way karate was written but also did the most to turn karate from a variety of different techniques taught in various places into a complete form. He changed the names of the many of the kata—the techniques students had to practice—and, influenced by his knowledge of kendo, introduced new ideas about distance and timing.

From here, karate developed in a number of different ways. Funakoshi's student, Hironori Ohtsuka, added more elements of kendo and a bit of jujitsu to create a freer and more practical martial arts form known as wado-ryu karate. The style most practiced in the United States though is isshin-ryu karate which means "one heart method" and was named in 1956. It was brought to America by marines stationed on Okinawa. Altogether, the World Karate Federation recognizes four different styles of karate and the World Union of Karate-do Organizations accepts eight.

To talk then of either judo or karate as a "traditional" martial art is to miss the point. Every martial art has an origin then develops in all sorts of different ways, adding new elements and changing techniques.

And martial arts should do that.

Every attack inspires a new defensive move, requiring martial arts masters to look for new ways to counter that defense and help their school to grow and develop. To keep a martial arts form static in the name of tradition would be irresponsible and perhaps even dangerous too. It would certainly be less enjoyable. One of the thrills of learning martial arts is that the learning never ends. There are always more moves to learn, more techniques to practice and more ways of defending against an attacker or overcoming an opponent.

When you're looking for a martial art to study then, tradition is important. It tells you something about the way you're going to be learning, how the school operates, whether it emphasizes defense or attack, grapples or strikes.

But the fact that it's been around for a long time or advertises itself as "traditional" shouldn't be the key factor that determines which martial art you choose.

It's more important to find a martial arts with a rich future than one with a solid tradition.

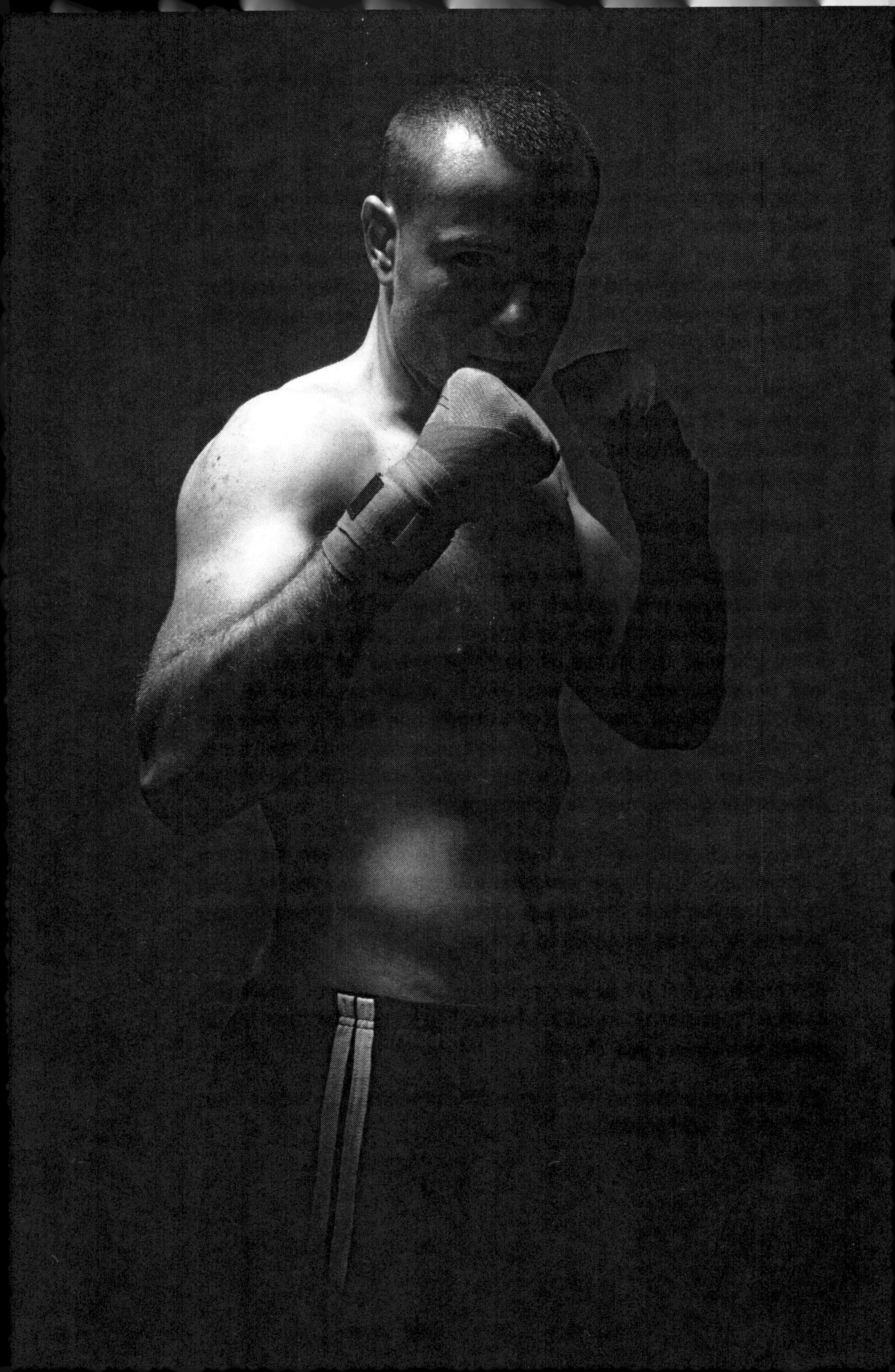

MYTH **4**

THE WEST HAS NO MARTIAL ARTS TRADITION OF ITS OWN

Martial arts can sometimes look mysterious. In fact, it's that mystery that often makes a school look so inviting. It's as though centuries of secret fighting knowledge have been handed down from generation to generation until they come to rest in a martial arts teacher, someone who is prepared to pass them on to a chosen student who is prepared to put in the effort and training to develop the skills. And yet, that only seems to apply Eastern martial arts. Not only do Western martial arts seem to lack that sense of mystery but because they don't have it, they're often ignored. Think of martial arts today, and you're much more likely to imagine kung fu, karate or aikido than any of Europe's own traditions.

Language might have something to do with it. Eastern martial arts use strange terms that students have to learn if they're going to understand their techniques. Learn the language—not something that's too demanding—and you'll already own some of a technique's secrets.

The habits and practices of Eastern martial arts can be strange too: you have to wear unusual clothes, perhaps bow to your teacher and show the kind of respect and obedience that you rarely find in the West these days.

All of these things now appear to be such a part of martial arts that forms that don't have them—such boxing or wrestling—aren't always seen as martial arts at all.

That's a shame because the West has a rich tradition of fighting techniques.

We've already seen how pankration was one of the world's oldest forms of martial arts with competitions between fighters who could wrestle as well as they could kick taking place more than two thousand years ago, and Greco-Roman wrestling dates back to the same era.

It's really in the medieval period though that European martial arts begin to take off as a form that's taught, mastered and used—often with fatal consequences.

The first master of European martial arts was the German Johannes Liechtenauer. He taught in the fourteenth century and many of the fencing manuals that date from that time are said to be derived from his techniques.

And that's perhaps that's the biggest difference between European martial arts and Eastern martial arts: while Eastern martial arts appear to place an emphasis on unarmed combat, the techniques that developed in Germany and France depend on weapons. They explain how to fight with a sword and buckler, a knife or short sword, a long sword or a quarterstaff. When those weapons became obsolete, there was little point in knowing how to use them in self-defense. Knowing how to joust might have been important if you were a knight with a horse, a squire and maiden you wanted to impress, but it's not much use if you're facing a mugger in a dark alley at night.

And sometimes weapons training isn't very complex. We've seen how Shaolin martial arts actually had little to do with copying animal movements to create fighting styles and much more to do with hitting people with a long stick. One Shaolin technique consists of little more than teaching students to use their long staff like a farmer digs a field: push the end of the stick down hard then pull it up fast to deliver a blow to the legs, groin or abdomen. Critics at the time thought it rudimentary but they also noted that it was easy to teach and very effective.

European armed fighting techniques tended to be a little more sophisticated, and the range of weapons taught was particularly broad. Dagger-fighting could have consisted of fighting with two daggers for example, or with rondel daggers—a kind of long, thin knife with a round handle, mostly used for stabbing through chain mail. Students would have practiced sword fighting with a dussack, a single-edged wooden sword without a hilt and an open grip like a scissors-handle.

Another difference between Eastern and Western martial arts though—and perhaps another reason why the popularity of Western martial arts has waned while Eastern martial arts has only grown—was the motivation for learning fighting skills.

China and Japan both suffered from a great deal of banditry, so there was demand among villagers to learn how to defend themselves from attack. Monks too often formed part of the Chinese empire's fighting forces. In Europe though, one of the main reasons that people wanted to learn to fight well was to survive duels. Trial by combat was part of the legal process in Germany and there are records dating back to the eighth century describing the way families disputing land ownership would touch soil from the property with their swords then battle it out to see who was right. The last trial by combat in England took place as late as 1583.

Duels too were held to preserve honor and German college students were famous for collecting scars. Knowing how to handle a sword was an important part of every gentleman's education, and without that knowledge, there was always a chance of injury or dishonor.

But none of that means that Europe didn't have its own tradition of unarmed combat as well. Perhaps the most famous unarmed combat technique is France's savate, a type of kickboxing. The word itself means "old shoe."

Modern martial arts schools might owe a lot to Eastern fighting techniques but if you want a form that's closer to home, there's plenty with a rich history to choose from including fencing, boxing and wrestling.

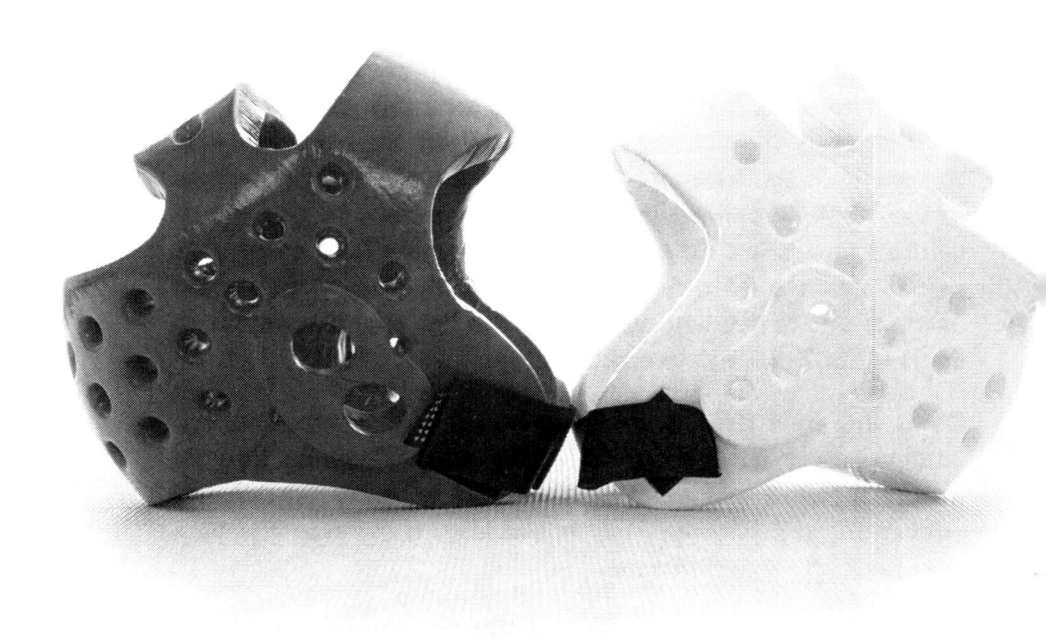

MYTH **5**

Martial Arts are Out of Date

Tradition is part of the appeal of martial arts. Learn kung fu, karate, judo or just about any other ancient fighting method and you're not just going to be practicing how to block kicks and disarm an opponent. You're also plugging in to hundreds of years of history. You'll be learning the skills of the ancient fighting masters and taking your warrior skills right from the source, from a time when all fighting took place hand-to-hand and man-to-man.

As we've seen, that's not always true. Martial arts do change. Masters develop new techniques and influences come in from other combat forms. But there is usually a core of techniques or at the very least, a certain approach, that let students feel that they're learning more than skills; they picking up a fighting tradition.

But tradition is a double-edged sword. While a traditional martial art will have a rich history and a strong identity, if it's traditional, won't it also be unchanging? And as the world changes, doesn't that mean that traditional martial arts are out of date?

At first glance, it might appear that there's something to this accusation. Few martial arts classes, for example, will spend a great deal of time talking about ways of defending yourself against a man with a gun. That's not surprising when you consider that most martial arts techniques were discovered at a time when the most dangerous thing someone might face would be a bandit with a stick, a knife or a sword at worst. It doesn't matter how well you control your qi, it's not going to be enough to stop a speeding bullet. There's little point in a martial arts school advertising the fact that after twelve years of hard training and enough black belts to fill a wardrobe, you're not going to be able to defend yourself against a twelve-year old with a Magnum and an expensive computer game addiction.

Look a little closer though, and the truth is very different. Many martial arts forms are indeed traditional but they're also dynamic, effective and yes, up to date too.

The most obvious way in which martial arts stay up to date is the completely new forms that crop up all the time. While fighters have always mixed their combat techniques, the Mixed Martial Arts' Ultimate Fighting Championship was only formed in 1993. And if that sounds untraditional, then think again. In its current form, mixed martial arts might be new but it can be traced back to Bruce Lee's jeet kune do. That form was a combination of all sorts of different martial arts, some of which had become rigid as point-based competitions turned them into sports instead of genuine fighting systems.

Krav maga too might now be used as the self-defense technique of the Israeli army, but it started as a way for Jews in Bratislava to defend themselves against anti-Semitic attacks. It's since been updated and made so useful that it's now a part of the basic training of a number of armed forces.

So although martial artists wear traditional clothing, take part in traditional rituals and call their moves by traditional names instead of simply calling them "high punch" or "low kick," it should be clear that they're also constantly changing with the times.

Not that they need to do that very much to remain effective and up to date. Ultimately, any decent martial arts system should always help someone to overcome an unarmed attacker or disarm a knife-wielding mugger. Martial arts might adapt and change, but muggers and other attackers change much less.

In the end, the ability of a martial arts technique to enable someone to defend themselves will always be the ultimate test of whether it's up to date or not—and you have to look hard to find a martial arts system that can't do that.

But it's not the only test. The main aim of martial arts might be self-defense but there are plenty of other benefits to be won from the regular practice of fighting moves, and they're things that never go out of style either.

The fact that practicing martial arts can keep people fit, for example, means that sparring, training and practice are more up to date than ever. When food was scarce and most work was manual, few people had to worry about being overweight or leading unhealthy lifestyles. Today's urban living though has made the need for regular exercise greater than ever.

Martial arts deliver that very modern need in a traditional way.

And martial arts training supplies discipline too. At a time when kids are faced with all sorts of temptations from video games and endless Internet surfing to gangs and drugs, the discipline of practicing moves until they're perfect, respecting their elders and teachers—because no martial arts teacher will accept back talk from a student in the way that high school teachers often do—couldn't be more timely or more needed.

Martial arts is traditional. It has customs that can be dated back centuries and moves that have been tested and found to be effective over many, many years. It's also flexible and adaptable. Martial arts forms that don't stand the test of time fade away or change into forms that will stand up to opponents.

Martial arts also continues to deliver many of the health and spiritual benefits that we need as much today as we've always done.

And finally, if martial arts fail to teach too many lessons on disarming gun-toting thieves, that's because those situations are, fortunately, relatively rare—and once you're up close to the attacker, they can also be overcome with many of the same moves used for any other kind of defense.

MYTH 6

THERE'S NO SUCH THING AS BAD MARTIAL ARTS

In 1984, movie production company MGM, who should really have known better, released *Gymkata*, a martial arts film starring Olympic gold medal-winning gymnast Kurt Thomas. Combining Eastern martial arts with the ability to somersault on wooden beams and swing from hoops, Thomas fights off bad guys to help the US win a savage fighting competition and place a piece of Star Wars machinery in the fictional state of Parmistan.

A few minutes in front of that film should be enough to convince anyone that there is indeed such a thing as bad martial arts.

But *Gymkata*, of course, is only a film,. There isn't really a form of martial arts in which the fighters must first learn to perform a back flip with a triple-twist before they can send a kick to the back of an attacker's head. Tae kwon do might involve lots of painful stretching, and capoeira can sometimes look more like dancing than fighting, but they're all based on combat techniques, they all deliver real benefits to the people who practice them, and they all have their own advantages. They're all good in their own way.

Bad martial arts—gymkata excluded—isn't about the fighting form itself. It's about the way the martial art is promoted, the way it's practiced and the way it's used.

People take up martial arts for all sorts of different reasons. Some people want to learn some simple techniques that will enable them to defend themselves against an attacker. They're less interested in the history of the form, the discipline, the spirituality or the tradition than in knowing a couple of simple blows that will get them out of trouble.

Other people want to master a form of martial arts. They want to know everything about it. They want to work their way up through the belts, explore the form's history and practice until each move is perfect. That's legitimate too.

But in every new class there is always at least one student whose main motivation seems to be to enjoy the pleasure of hitting someone. They don't just get a kick out of kicking, they get a kick out of kicking someone.

That's not legitimate. It's not that the martial arts itself is bad, but the wrong motivation will lead to bad martial arts practice.

And that applies to all forms of martial arts. Choose the wrong kind of martial arts for the goals you want to achieve, and even if the form itself isn't bad, it will be bad for you.

It's not just students who have to consider how they want to use the skills they're learning. Martial arts teachers also need to be sure that they don't exploit the people who come to them seeking knowledge.

This is perhaps the worst kind of martial arts but it does crop up every now and then. A martial arts teacher will promise to reveal the thousand-year old secrets of some little known martial arts form that will enable anyone to floor an opponent with a look, kill with a finger poke or pack unbelievable power into their kicks.

Or they'll say that they've discovered a fantastic method to add muscle mass, improve stamina or develop "rock-solid" stances that no one can knock over.

And all of that information can be yours by buying this ebook for $19.95 or by attending a workshop at which places are limited and the fees in triple figures.

In the end, you'll learn nothing that you couldn't have picked up during the beginner's class at just about every martial arts school, and you won't be told anything the guy at the counter selling whey powder wouldn't say. Although you might have picked up a neat lesson in marketing skills that lots of other people possess.

Again, this doesn't mean that martial arts is bad or that particular form of martial arts is bad. It just means that martial arts teacher is bad, and is more interested in turning a buck than in teaching students skills they can use.

Sometimes though, the willingness of students to believe in the impossible has nothing to do with a teacher's desire to make some extra cash. The attraction of martial arts is its ability to enable people who learn it to do things that other people can't do. That might be as simple as blocking a knife attack but over time, stories have also cropped up suggesting that martial arts experts can levitate over attackers or paralyze not with a blow but with a secret combination of finger pushes.

These are stories that have more to do with motion pictures than with real martial arts. They don't make martial arts bad but they do make for bad ideas about martial arts—and that's the kind of thing that will lead to disappointment, poor training and poor results.

Martial arts is a tool. It's a tool that comes in many forms, shapes and sizes, each one of which does something slightly different. None of those forms is bad but if you don't use the right form for the right job—or if a teacher makes claims about a form that aren't true—then the use of that martial arts will never be right.

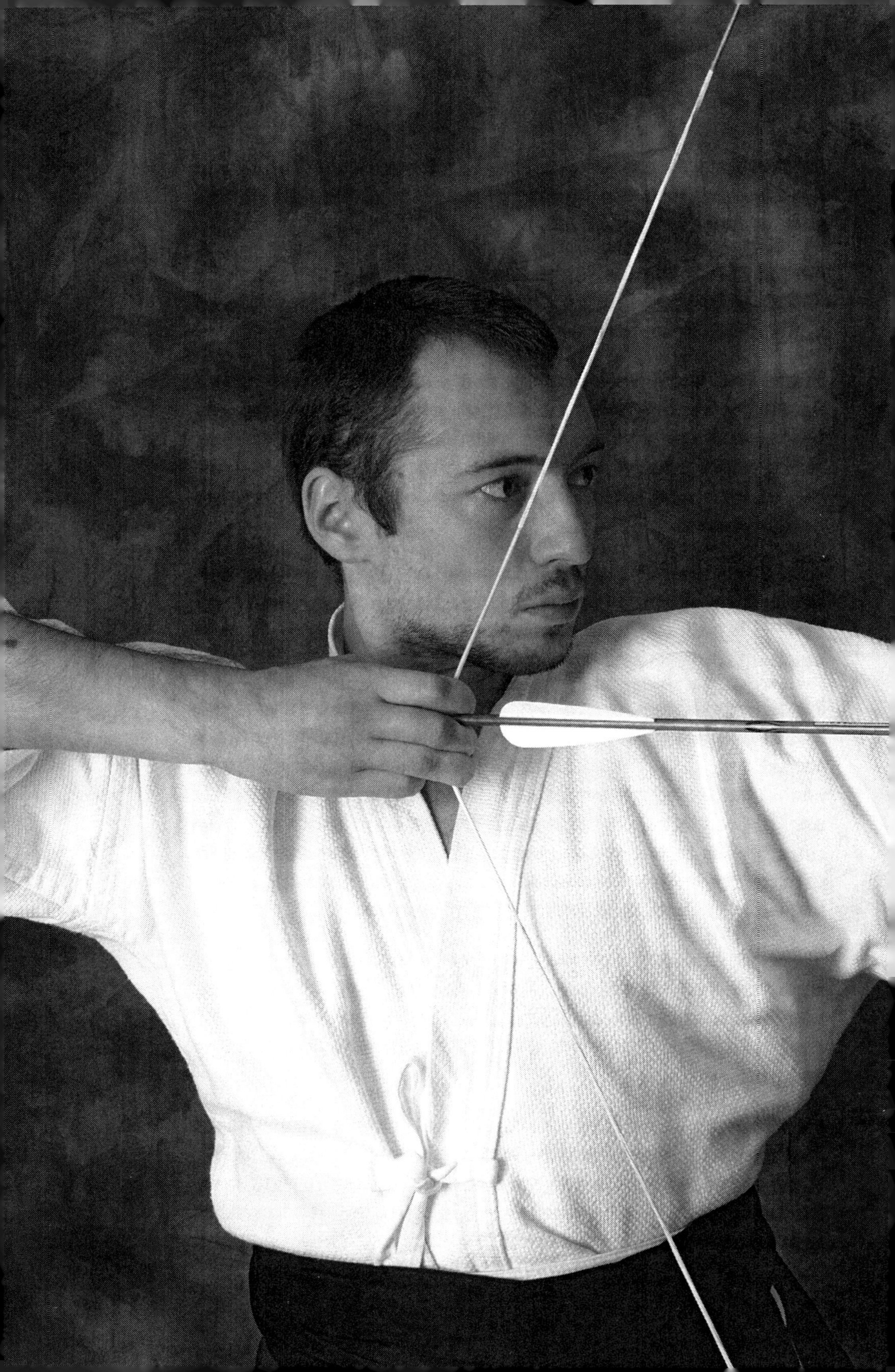

MYTH **7**

MARTIAL ARTS IS ALL ABOUT WINNING FIGHTS

While the variety of different martial arts forms have many origins, for most techniques, the starting point is the military. Alexander the Great trained his forces in pankration before they began their march towards India. Gatka, a Sikh martial art form which requires the simultaneous use of two weapons and is performed accompanied by music and singing, is believed to be derived from an Indian military training course called shaster vidiya. And Genghis Khan used bkyukl bökh, another form of wrestling, to keep his troops ready for battle.

When you're training with the knowledge that not only will you definitely need the skills you're learning but that you will actually be using them to fight for your life, you tend to spar with the aim of thoroughly beating the other guy. Fail to use your martial arts skills to win fights in those days and you'd have found find that losing carries a very high price.

It's no wonder then that martial arts certainly have the impression of being all about winning fights.

Even today, when most martial arts students can afford to take their training a little less seriously, many techniques appear to be geared towards dominating others, winning submissions and battling opponents. That's particularly true of those martial arts that have now become sports. The consequences of defeat might not be as serious as those faced by an ancient Greek soldier or a Mongol warrior who has allowed an enemy to get the better of him, but the first goal of a martial arts athlete is still to win a bout—and that can only be achieved by overpowering and defeating an opponent.

For judokas, boxers and fencers then, the rewards of victory might not be as valuable as the chance to live and fight again, but an Olympic medal is still a pretty impressive prize to battle for, and it can only be won by standing in front of an opponent and beating him or her face-to-face.

So it does look as though martial arts really is all about winning fights. That was what martial arts was about thousands of years ago, and even though the most common fights might have moved to the gym rather than the battlefield, that's what they're about today.

Look a little closer though, and you can see there's a lot more to it than that.

Archery, for example, is a form of martial arts. It requires discipline, training and the skilful use of a traditional weapon. But success at archery is never measured by fighting opponents. No two archers will ever be asked to face each other thirty yards apart at the Olympic games and invited to see who can shoot first and most accurately. Instead, the skill is measured by their ability to hit a static target. The opponent they're fighting then isn't the person standing next to them at the competition; it's their potential to be distracted, to lose focus and to allow their arm to lose its stability.

If archery is about beating an opponent, that opponent is the fighter him- or herself.

That's true of the vast majority of martial arts today. While many students are motivated by the desire to be able to protect themselves if necessary—to win a fight that they've been forced to take part in—few will ever actually put their skills to the test in that way. They want to be able to win if they have to, but if that's the only aim of their martial arts practice, then they're likely to find their training a pretty hollow and unsatisfying experience.

The real aim of martial arts is usually to identify and beat your own limitations.

The structure of dans and belts provides students with a way to do that. They can always see the next challenge to overcome, understand what they have to do to beat it, and enjoy the rewards of their efforts before preparing for their next step up.

If martial arts were only about beating others, then the skills wouldn't be laid out in a series of lessons in which you have to master some before you can move onto the others. The strongest and most effective moves would always be taught immediately and the course would end there. Students would already understand everything they need to know.

Practitioners of internal martial arts forms too are rarely motivated by the desire to win a fight. They're looking to relax, to enjoy a few moments of calm and meditation, and in doing so, to improve their health and wellbeing.

And then, of course, there are the many young students today who take up martial arts in order to give themselves something constructive and useful to do after school that doesn't involve sitting in front of a computer screen or hanging out at the mall.

On the one hand then, it certainly is true that martial arts is about winning fights but those fights are rarely those in which two people face each other and test their martial skills. Only a small fraction of martial artists, after all, take part in competitive bouts and sparring is usually about practicing moves rather than beating a partner.

Self-defense is about winning fights. You learn the skills you need to stop a man with a knife or a group of attackers, and then you stop.

Martial arts is about learning a skill and overcoming challenges within yourself. They deliver a victory that can't be achieved any other way and one which is so much more valuable.

MYTH **8**

MARTIAL ARTS IS ALL ABOUT SPIRITUALITY

The practice of martial arts can be something of a paradox. On the one hand, the goal is clearly physical and usually violent. The moves and techniques have been designed specifically to harm—and even kill—someone else. Even those martial arts forms that are more defensive than aggressive, that place greater emphasis on giving way and deflecting blows than punching and kicking, still recognize that to end an attack, a martial artist has to be able to strike back.

Martial arts might not be all about winning fights, but it would be wrong to say that beating opponents and attackers is not an important aspect of combat training.

And yet, there's also another side to martial arts. Many of the people who practice a martial art say they have no intention of ever getting involved in a fight. They'll argue that the violent aspects of the technique that they're learning are a coincidence, something left over from the tradition's origins. The moves might, in theory, be able to help them beat off an attacker but that's not the reason they're learning and it's not what keeps them learning.

There's something to that argument. Few muggers know anything about martial arts. Most rely on fear, a knife and the fact that handing over a wallet is much less dangerous than fighting to keep it. For most people then, a few simple self-defense moves, such as knowing some weak points to kick or the most sensitive spots to insert a finger, should be enough to protect themselves. Martial arts clearly then has much more to offer than simple self-defense.

Discipline and the satisfaction of overcoming a physical challenge are certainly some aspects of that, but spirituality has always played an important part in martial arts as well.

The most famous example is probably the arrival of Bodhidarma, an Indian monk also known as Da Mo, at the Shaolin temple in the sixth century to teach Zen Buddhism. According to legend, Bodhidarma saw that the temple's monks lacked the stamina to meditate properly so he taught them a series of yogic exercises that later formed the foundation of kung fu.

How much of that story is true is debatable but it is known that a monk called Da Mo did live at the Shaolin temple and was Temple Master between 512 and 527 AD. He also created a dynamic tension exercise called "18 Lohan Hands" which was later published as the *Yi Jin Jing*.

The link between Buddhism—a non-violent, vegetarian belief system—and martial arts then might look strange but it's certainly there. And part of that connection lies in the belief of the existence of qi. The word itself can mean different things at different times and in different contexts but for martial artists, it refers to a kind of life-force, an energy that can be channeled through the body. Mastering qi is said to allow a martial artist to increase the power of his blows, and disrupting the flow of qi in an opponent's body is said to be able cause injury or even death.

It's the same belief that lies behind acupuncture which is said to stimulate the "meridians" along which the qi flows. Placing the needles in the correct places is supposed to unblock flow and restore balance to a sick person's body.

The type of martial arts that draws most heavily on the belief in qi is, of course, tai chi. A form of qi gong, "qi techniques," the slow moves of tai chi are intended to channel the qi, creating a sense of harmony and improving the body's health.

Other forms of qi gong include min zin, a Burmese martial art whose aims are to control negative thoughts and create a sense of balance, and bando yoga, another Burmese form in which practitioners hope to defend themselves against both external physical attack and internal disease while leading a life free from confrontation. Some of these ideas can also be found in the new Korean form, kuk sool won.

It's not just qi, and it's not just Chinese martial arts that have a spiritual side though. At around 3,000 years old, kalarippayattu is one of the world's most ancient martial arts forms and is centered on religion. The kalari, or gym, acts as a shrine to a number of different deities, including Shiva and Bhagavathi, and training begins with prayer and offerings. Even the warm-up is done facing the main shrine.

So there's certainly no question that spirituality is important for many forms of martial arts. But the degree to which it's important varies widely. Krav maga has no spiritual aspects at all; it's concerned solely with self-defense. Mixed martial arts too is only about beating an opponent, even if it is done in the ring—or a cage. And boxing, kickboxing and wrestling are also athletic martial arts whose only spiritual benefits are the discipline of training, steady improvement and overcoming challenges both physical and mental.

Much has been said and written about the spiritual aspects of martial arts, and it's something that's been caricatured in Hollywood movies and Hong Kong martial arts films too. Part of that may be the result of the popularity of Shaolin martial arts. If kung fu developed in a monastery, then its masters have access to supernatural secrets that only be revealed through proper martial arts training.

Kung fu is just one kind of martial art and not every type

concerns itself with spirituality. One of the benefits of having such a huge range of different martial arts forms to choose from is that students can find a technique with the level of spirituality to suit them.

Martial artists who want to keep their qi in harmony can learn tai chi or one of the other qi gong forms. Those looking to focus solely on fighting skills can study one of the more modern schools that place an emphasis on overcoming opponents.

MYTH 9

MARTIAL ARTS INCREASES AGGRESSIVENESS IN ITS STUDENTS

People who take up martial arts must be aggressive. Karate, judo and tae kwon do might all touch on spirituality, they might all pay lip-service to the idea of non-violence, discipline and control, but even if they're not solely about hitting people then violence and aggression is certainly a key element of the training.

If you're going to practice being aggressive, then it stands to reason that the result will be that martial arts students actually become more aggressive.

It's an idea backed up by some psychological theory. The concept of social learning suggests that when people see others get what they want by using a certain method, they're likely to use that methods themselves. If a kid growing up in gang-ridden neighborhood, for example, sees a drug dealer roll up in a fancy car, he'll understand that to get a fancy car, he needs to be a drug dealer too.

In martial arts then, students should quickly learn that aggression leads to victory—and that if they want to be effective martial artists, they need to increase their aggressiveness.

It's understandable. But it's also completely wrong. A number of studies have shown that not only does practicing martial arts not increase aggressiveness, it can actually reduce the chances that someone will respond to a situation violently.

T.A. Nosanchuk, a sociologist at Carleton University in Canada, has conducted several experiments to measure the effect of martial arts training on aggression and has repeatedly found that the longer a student performs martial arts, the *lower* their level of aggression falls. This was true across a number of different fighting forms. It might be expected that aggression in karatekas and students of tae kwon do, which focus on striking objects and blocking blows, might drop but in a study of 51 students, the same result was also seen among judokas, regardless of sex.

Other studies have found similar results: the more a martial artist trains and further they rise up the belt levels, the lower their "assaultive hostility"—the tendency to respond to a situation with physical violence.

A number of reasons have been put forward to explain what looks like a surprising result.

John R. Suler, a psychoanalyst and author of *Contemporary Psychoanalysis and Eastern Thought*, argues that martial arts training raises self-esteem, heightens confidence, increases empathy, provides a sense of peacefulness and improves wellbeing. As a martial artist trains, he argues, the student becomes more aware of the emotions of his opponents. That allows him to spot rising anger in others early and deflect situations that could lead to violence.

A calm, peaceful teacher too can provide a model of non-aggression for students to copy and follow, and while some training routines do include sparring—which could increase aggression—Suler says, most focus on practicing kata. Repeating those moves can become a form of meditation, giving the practitioner a sense of self-control. The fact the techniques are said to date back hundreds of years and are performed surrounded by others in the context of a dojo also gives martial artists a sense of belonging and confidence. All of that can help to remove feelings of weakness and insecurity that can lead someone to respond aggressively.

Nosanchuk agrees. He claims that martial arts improves four areas which together reduce someone's tendency to be aggressive: self-control, self-assertiveness, self-esteem, and self-confidence.

All of this research has at least one problem though: martial artists are a self-selective bunch. People choose to take up martial arts for a range of different reasons and those who do choose to study a martial arts because they want to get a thrill out of hitting people are unlikely to stay in judo, karate or tae kwon do, the forms most studied by researchers. Martial arts schools can have a high dropout rate and it's possible that the most aggressive people leave the forms that emphasize non-aggression and take up some of the more violent forms.

On the whole though, this all looks like good news. Practicing martial arts—like practicing any sports—can provide an emotional outlet.

The training can improve confidence. A good teacher can provide an excellent role model for young students. And learning to master moves and rise up the belt ranks improves self-esteem, all of which make people less violent.

But there is one drawback. All of these benefits are only felt by the people who practice martial arts. For people who watch martial arts, the opposite can happen. Researchers have found that watching aggressive sports—such as ice hockey—increases aggression. (The same effect isn't seen when people watch non-aggressive sports). One researcher even found that murder rates rise in the USA after heavyweight title boxing matches and that the types of murders mirror the fight: when a white boxer lost, more white men were killed; when a black boxer lost, more black men were murdered.

The moral then should be clear: to reduce aggression, practice martial arts and continue practicing it, don't just sit and watch it.

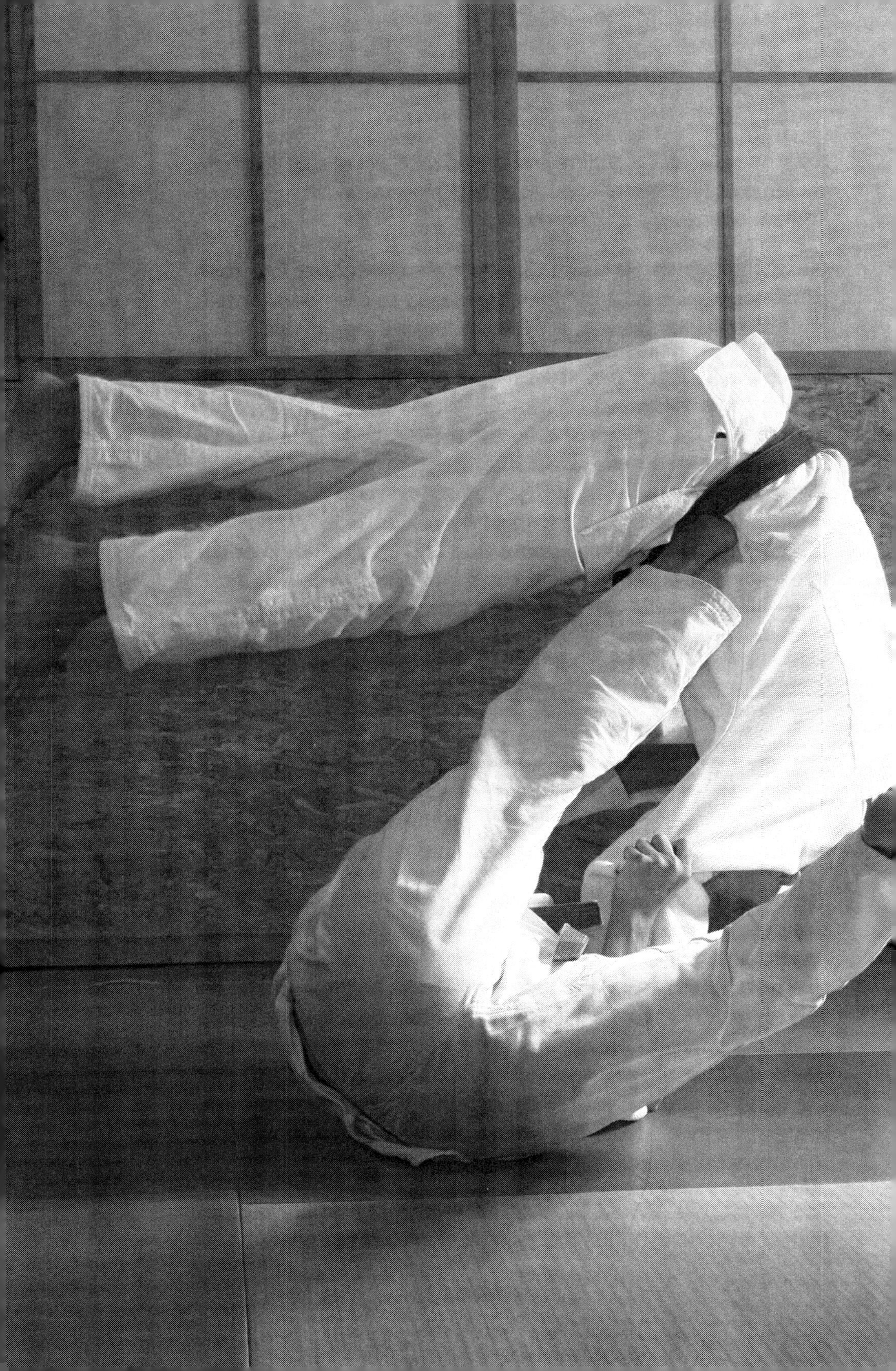

MYTH **10**

Martial Arts is a Sport and Has Nothing to Do with Real Fighting

To become a true martial artist, you'll have to spend a great deal of time training. Some of that time will be spent sparring but depending on the forms you're learning, it's likely that much of it will also involve learning kata. Time and again, you'll practice moves and combinations of moves that appear to have little to do with fighting.

You'll practice your stance, advance in unusual ways and learn how to fall over, when want you really wanted to learn is how to make the other guy fall over.

And you'll do it all while wearing odd clothes, calling your teacher "sifu" and treating any opponent you might have with the utmost respect.

Then you'll step out of a bar, run into a bunch of guys who will treat you with anything but respect and beat you silly because, instead of learning how to defend yourself, you were too busy channeling your qi and pretending you were Bruce Lee.

Or so many critics of martial arts would have you believe. Martial arts, they say, is nice and traditional and cultural and fun. It's a good after-school activity, and some forms might make decent competitive sports but they've got nothing to do with self-defense and even less to do with winning the kinds of fights you can come across in the streets.

At first sight, there might be something to this. There are some pretty obvious and important differences between martial arts bouts and real street fights.

First, street fights are surprising. If you knew that going to a particular place at a particular time was going to have you fighting for your life, you'd go somewhere else. It can take just seconds for a situation to develop from a look or a bump into insults and drawn knives. That's not enough time to think about your moves, remember your kata, draw a deep breath and focus your qi. If you're lucky, you'll just have enough time to see the knife.

And that knife is going to be a lot closer than you're used to in a martial arts classes. Sparring and sports competitions take place at set distances so that neither side starts with an advantage. Part of the build-up to a fight often involves closing down that distance so that one side starts with an advantage. An attacker will often deliberately invade the defender's space, challenging him to launch the first attack or demanding that he give away an important position before the fight has even begun. You'll have no more than a second to decide which you're going to do.

There's also a very good chance that attacker challenging you to a fight will be bigger than you—and there's likely to be lots of them. Attackers do have a habit of traveling in packs and they rarely pick on people bigger and more numerous than them. To a judoka used to starting a bout with his hands carefully placed on the uniform of a single opponent in the same weight band, that's all going to look very unfamiliar.

Nor will it get easier should the judoka or tae kwon do expert manage to throw his opponent to the ground and begin grappling. In a gym, no one is going to come the opponent's help until he submits. On the street, hit the floor and you'll soon find that your attacker's friends think you're at the perfect height for kicking.

And most importantly of all, sparring and sports fights have their limitations. Lose a fight in a competition or in a workout and you'll be disqualified or lose face. That's not pleasant but no one will have died. That's not necessarily true of a street fight, a fact which brings an unfamiliar degree of fear and a level of adrenaline a martial artist used to training in a gym won't have felt before.

On the one hand then, it shouldn't take much more than a quick look at a typical street fight to see that there's a world of difference between martial arts and plain fighting. But that doesn't mean that knowledge of martial arts isn't helpful in a street fight.

Training in martial arts will certainly help to improve reaction time and enable a defender to block blows, however close they are when they're delivered. Street fighters tend to spend little time defending themselves, preferring instead to overcome their opponent with a quick flurry of punches and kicks. Survive that with some simple blocks or throws and they'll often have exhausted themselves and their ideas. If they can't beat you right away, there's a good chance that they'll beat it right away. You might not get to find out what your roundhouse kick can do in practice but the defensive moves you learn in a martial arts class—often the bulk of early lessons—can put you in good stead if you need them. They'll do what self-defense is supposed to do: enable you to defend yourself against attack.

If you do find yourself needing to hit though then clearly not all of the moves you know are going to be appropriate. But they're not meant to be. A good martial artist should know which technique to use when. If the attacker is close then a high kick won't be very effective but a jab to a sensitive point might be. A fight between a martial artist and a street fighter will never be as stylish, as fair or as easy on the eyes as a sports competition or sparring in the gym. It will be short and brutal. But a skilled martial artist—even one with no experience in real fighting battling a seasoned fighter—should be able to use his or her skills to *at least* survive the attack without suffering too much harm.

But the biggest benefit that martial arts can bring to a street fight is that they make the fight less likely. We've already seen that the more someone trains in martial arts, the more confident and the less aggressive they become. For martial artists, difficult situations rarely occur because attackers are put off by their calm and confidence—and knowing that the defender knows how to defend himself means that they're more likely to leave you well alone. As Bruce Lee said: "If you don't fight, you cannot lose."

MYTH **11**

TRUE MARTIAL ARTS IS ALWAYS UNARMED

Defending yourself against an attack is very easy. You don't need to spend years practicing kata. You don't have to join a dojo, wear pajamas or bow to a teacher. You can simply buy a revolver small enough to stick in a pocket or hide in a handbag.

As long as you can whip it out fast enough, have the nerve to hold it without shaking and can shoot straight enough to stop an attacker, then you won't need to how to block, grapple or roundhouse kick.

All of that though is a big if. Attackers rarely give their victims time to reach for their weapons, let alone load them, and guns have little to do with martial arts which teach a whole range of different fighting skills. Martial arts students usually want to know more than how to defend themselves. They also want to practice a sport, match themselves against an opponent and take part in a challenging physical activity. Often that means putting weapons aside and focusing on unarmed combat. It certainly means putting a gun away.

But the origin of almost all martial arts is military. Today's armed forces might focus on using rifles, explosives and all sorts of other technological tools but when the moves now taught in martial arts schools were being developed, they were intended for use by soldiers, travelers and monks who had access to a wide range of weapons from walking staffs to spears and halberds. Most of those weapons are no longer in use but they still form a vital part of many of the world's leading martial arts forms.

Shaolin martial arts, for example, has "18 Arms of Wushu." The list varies but includes an impressive range of different types of weapons divided into five categories: long, short, soft, rare and hidden.

The staff is the most important, largely because it was available anywhere, was easy to carry and its use as a walking stick meant that it didn't arouse suspicion. But there are also 36 different kinds of two-sectioned staffs—the kind in which the two parts are attached by a chain—as well as three-sectioned staffs. Those are fairly familiar, especially to fans of kung fu films, but the Shaolin arsenal also includes a *gou*, a kind of long, narrow hook with a sharp point at both ends, used mainly for disarming opponents; the *zi-wu*, a curved knuckleduster with two points shaped like deer horns; *chiu*, a pair of round-headed mallets; the monk's spade, a kind of flat, broad-headed spear; a nine-sectioned steel whip, a long chain with a dart on the end used to keep attackers at bay, as well all sorts of swords and double-daggers for experienced fighters.

It's not just Shaolin though whose fighters know what to do with weapons. The use of combat tools is spread right across different martial arts forms in different parts of the world.

In India, which in kalarippayattu might well have the world's oldest continuously taught martial arts form, weapons usually include swords, sticks and daggers in a number of different forms. The *cheruvadi* or *muchen*, for example, is a plain staff three palm-lengths long. The *gadha* is a kind of round-headed mace and the *otta* is a curved wooden tool shaped like an elephant's trunk. Daggers include the *jambiya*, a curved knife worn on a belt, the *bich'hwa*, named after the scorpion with a double-edge and two curves, and a number of short-bladed instruments held with the blade pointing out of the knuckles and used in a punching action. Kalarippayattu itself is perhaps best known for its use of swords and shields.

Pencak silat, an Indonesian martial arts form, uses *cabang*, a three-pointed knife that probably derives from the trident; *sabit*, a sickle-shaped tool that can be used for blocking, striking and slashing; *kerambit*, a short curved blade that women have been known to hide in their hair; and of course, the *keris*, a wavey knife washed in acid that's also used in religious ceremonies.

And weapons in martial arts aren't limited to the Far East. The history of European martial arts is a history of swordsmanship. Jousting with long poles might have been left in the history books but fencing with swords remains and is now an Olympic sport with three different kind of swords used: epees are heavy swords that can be used to stab anywhere on the body; foils are light swords also used for stabbing but whose target is limited to the torso; and sabres are slashing swords whose fencers use the edge to hit an opponent anywhere above the waist, even on the head.

So to say that true martial is always unarmed is completely wrong. In fact, martial arts from Europe to the Far East have a long tradition of using weapons that range from knives and daggers to chains and darts.

It is true though that few of these weapons skills are taught today, and perhaps for obvious reasons. Self-defense is an important motivation for people to take up martial arts today, and swords, halberds and three-sectioned staffs are neither self-defense weapons nor very practical ones. Even teaching someone how to use a knife isn't particularly popular in martial arts schools. Students usually want to know how to defend themselves against the sort of people who like to pack knives, not join them.

And there's the real problem of having to explain to a police officer why you're carrying a sharp weapon, whether it's legal or not.

The kind of weapons once used in martial arts are rarely sold today, which is also why they're rarely taught. But they are an important part of the history of martial arts and the challenge of practicing those techniques and the beauty of watching them does make them worth learning when possible.

MYTH **12**

ONE MARTIAL ARTS FORM IS BETTER THAN ALL THE OTHERS

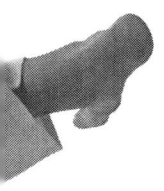

The best form of martial arts is one that avoids fights in the first place. But if you do want to start a scrap, you don't have to do any more than ask a room full of martial artists from a number of different disciplines which they think is the best.

A specialist from a northern kung fu school like chang quan or xingyi quan will say that his skills are the most powerful. He'll point out that his ability to kick fast, leap high and move with the agility of a tiger means that he's hard to hit but that his legs are lethal weapons.

A southern kung fu specialist—a student of bak mei or wing chun—would not be impressed. He'd say that his solid stance, strong arm and deft strikes mean that his northern neighbor's kicks would hardly affect him and that he'd be able to punch back hard.

A student of tae kwon do though would shake his head at both of them. Neither of those disciplines, he'd say, would be a match for his school. Even if they managed to land one blow, he'd soon be able to throw them on the floor where their punches and kicks would be ineffective and his holds would quickly have them begging for mercy.

The kung fu masters would together agree that the tae kwon do expert would never get close enough to either of them to practice his throws. A punch or a kick from either of them would disorient him too much and give them the fight. And so the argument would continue.

Every martial arts form is different. Each places a different emphasis on a particular aspect of fighting and self-defense, and each downplays those parts which it considers less important. For judokas, for example, martial arts is all about throws, holds and groundwork. For kung fu artists, on the other hand, the ground is just a launch pad for high-flying leaps and balanced thrusts.

And because different martial arts emphasize different fighting aspects so each leaves itself open to weaknesses that a knowledgeable fighter from another discipline might be able to exploit. In practice, when that happens the martial arts form adjusts. Judo, for example, developed from jujutsu when its founder Kano Jigoro decided to bring together jujutsu's different techniques and improve their efficiency. He stopped teaching jujutsu techniques that used force and emphasized moves that made use of balance, momentum and leverage.

And so a new martial arts was formed, one which took what Kano saw as the best elements of the traditional form, rejected the less effective moves and produced a stronger set of moves.

Perhaps the clearest example of this attempt to combine the best parts of different martial arts though is the rise of mixed martial arts.

As we've seen, combining different martial arts forms isn't new but the founding of the Ultimate Fighting Championship marked a real attempt to bring together a number of different types of martial arts in one full-contact sports championship.

If the kung fu specialists were masters of staying upright, punching and kicking, and judokas were experts at groundwork, mixed martial artists would be masters at both types of fighting.

So the stand-up part of a bout would draw on techniques from kickboxing, muay Thai, karate and boxing. The clinch would use moves drawn from Greco-Roman wrestling and judo among others, and once the opponent was on the floor Brazilian jujitsu and other wrestling techniques could be used to force a submission.

A mixed martial arts fighter would then have different coaches, each specializing in a different type of combat.

In theory then, mixed martial arts, a form which takes the best parts of a number of different martial arts forms should be the best. It should be the one with the fewest weaknesses and the most comprehensive range of fighting techniques.

In practice, of course, becoming a jack of all trades means that you're a master of none. A mixed martial arts fighter won't be as good at kicking or punching as a boxing or muay Thai specialist, and once on the floor, a trained judoka would likely have him submitting in no time at all. Mixed martial arts rely on the fact that their opponents are also generalists, rather than specialists who can beat them clearly in one aspect of the fight.

And then there are the weights. The fact that mixed martial arts has different weight classifications, like boxing, suggests that it's not a technique that anyone can use to defeat any attacker. While someone who knows mixed martial arts should be able to defend himself against someone who knows no martial arts, he might well struggle against a trained attacker who is bigger than him.

That's a weakness that wouldn't be ignored by the kung fu specialists who would claim that with their techniques, height and weight don't matter; discipline, control and use of qi are far more important influences on power.

No one martial arts is better than any other. But no one who practices martial arts is likely to believe that.

Or at least to admit it.

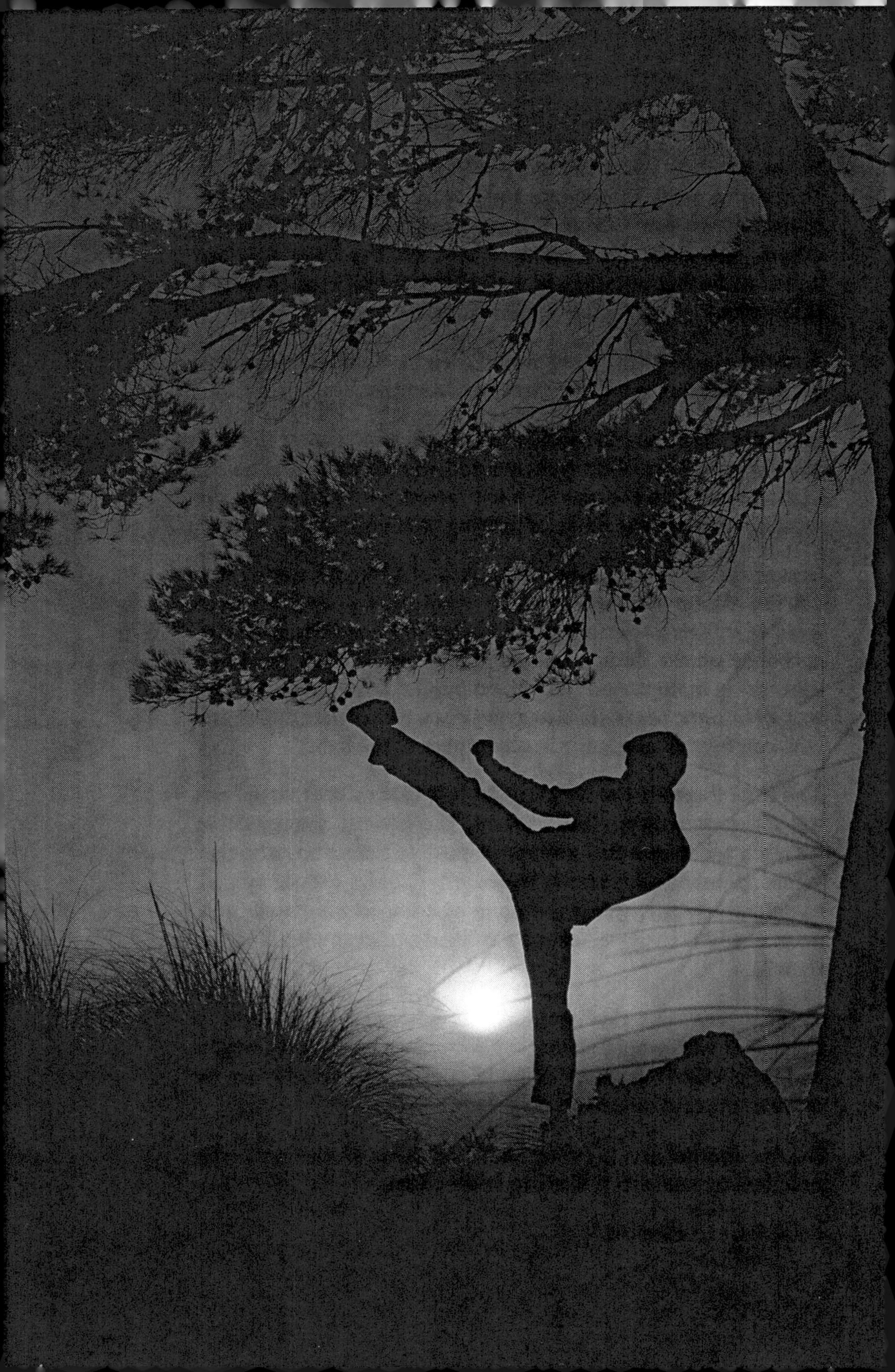

MYTH **13**

ONE FIGHTER IS BETTER THAN ALL THE OTHERS

If asking a group of martial artists from a range of different disciplines which form of martial arts is the best doesn't start a giant argument, there's another question you can ask. Demand that they name the world's best fighter and you'll get a list of names.

What you won't get is any agreement.

Today, for example, many would claim that Fedor Emelianenko is the world's best fighter. A mixed martial artist from Ukraine, Emelianenko has held five major championships: the Rings World Heavyweight Championships; the King of Kings Championships; The Pride World Heavyweight Championship; The Heavyweight Grand Prix Championships; and the World Alliance of Mixed Martial Arts Heavyweight Championship. ESPN and a number of specialist fighting publications have consistently named Emelianenko the best heavyweight fighter in the world, and many experts consider him to be the greatest martial artist ever.

Emelianenko started his martial arts career with judo and sambo, a self-defense regime created in the Soviet Union that combines judo with near eastern wrestling techniques. By the age of 25, he had added skills in striking and kicking, training with a team made up of a grappling coach, boxing coach and muay Thai coach. His professional record in mixed martial arts competitions consists of 30 fights, one no contest and one defeat—a controversial judge's decision in which an accidental blow from his opponent's elbow opened an old cut.

There's no question that Emelianenko is a strong and talented fighter. But is he the best in the world?

Mixed martial arts is a sport. It might be a particularly violent and brutal one, and it's intended to replicate as much as possible the real circumstances of a street fight. But it has rules. It has a ring that limits movement and it has weight restrictions that prevent people of different sizes from testing themselves against each other.

As often as people say that Emelianenko is the best fighter in the world, they also say that he's the best pound-for-pound fighter in the world, which isn't quite the same thing.

And many people too will say that mixed martial arts isn't a genuine martial arts at all. It's a new mixture of different techniques cannibalized from other martial arts forms rather than a tradition of its own. It has no history, no original moves and is more of a sport than an art.

Whether that's true or not, those martial artists with a more traditional outlook are likely to name a very different kind of warrior as the world's greatest fighter.

Bruce Lee was born in San Francisco in 1940, moving with his family to Hong Kong at the age of just three months. His mother Grace was a member of one of the island's wealthiest families; his father was an actor and Cantonese opera singer.

Lee started learning wing chun kung fu at the age of 13, training alone and with two friends after the rest of the school refused to spar with him because of his mother's part-German ancestry. In 1959, he moved back to the United States where he taught his own version of wing chun, which he called "jun fan gung fu," based on his Chinese name Lee Jun Fan. Later, Lee would adapt this form to create jeet kune do ("The Way of the Intercepting Fist"), a form which he considered "a style of no style." Jeet kune do's aim was to break out of the formalized approach of wing chun to create a new style that was practical, flexible and fast.

Above all, fast. At just 140-145 pounds, Lee was never going to be among the most powerful of fighters (although his emphasis on bodybuilding and fitness meant that he was capable of doing one-handed, two-finger push-ups and could hold a 125-pound barbell horizontally). But his speed was legendary. It was said that he was capable of delivering a blow from hands placed at his side within five hundredths of a second, could snatch a dime from an open hand and leave a penny behind before the hand could be closed, and was capable of catching rice grains thrown in the air using chopsticks. He was so agile that it was said he could perform leg lifts with only his shoulder blades resting on the edge of a bench.

To ask which, if any, of those stories is true is to miss the point. Bruce Lee, like Fedor Emelianenko, was clearly a talented and knowledgeable fighter. He create a revolutionary new martial arts system that was both practical and traditional, and trained many of the world's top martial artists, including Chuck Norris and Joe Lewis, two karate champions who themselves are often named in the list of the world's greatest all time fighters.

But Bruce Lee never competed professionally. He might have killed Chuck Norris in a famous showdown in the Rome Coliseum but there's a difference between a choreographed film fight and a real competition.

And there's a difference too between a competition and a street fight.

It may well be that there is one fighter who is greater than all the others. It may be too that that fighter is Fedor Emelianenko or Bruce Lee. Or it could be Chuck Norris, Joe Lewis or even Jean-Claude Van Damme.

But as long as there are different fighting forms, each with its own strengths and weaknesses, we'll never know who that fighter is. We'll just get to enjoy arguing about it.

MYTH 14

KUNG FU IS THE MOST POPULAR MARTIAL ART

If we can't say which is the best martial arts form, then surely we can say which is the most popular. It's just a matter of adding up all the numbers and calculating which branch of martial arts has the most practitioners.

If only it were that easy. Martial arts is a worldwide phenomenon practiced from Mongolia to Michigan and from South Africa to Scandinavia. Some of those forms are indigenous and unique, practiced only in those countries. Evala, for example, is a form of wrestling practiced by the Kabye people of Togo. It's the second part of a manhood ritual that starts with climbing three mountains and ends with circumcision. It's not something that's caught on worldwide.

It's hard though to find a country in which a judoka wouldn't be able to pick up a sparring partner.

But not all judo clubs and teachers are affiliated to a national organization that collects figures and statistics about the number of students at each school. And at what point would you count the numbers? Because people who take up martial arts do it for a wide range of different reasons, they drop out at different times too.

If one country has a tendency to open classes at the same time each year—the start of the school year, for example—then it's likely that a count of students made in September would be far higher than one made at the end of the school year.

And then there's the question of how to categorize the different sub-branches of martial arts. Falun gong has claimed to have more than 100 million practitioners in 114 countries. Its moves appear similar to those of internal martial arts forms such as tai chi, but it promotes itself as a health and spiritual movement rather than a form of self defense. If falun gong's practitioners are hoping to defend themselves against anything, then it's likely to be nothing more than ill health and a Chinese government worried about its popularity in China.

But if falun gong can't be counted as a martial art, then can tai chi itself? If not, then one potentially leading candidate for the world's most popular form of martial arts is out of the running.

And if it can be counted as a form of martial arts, then how are we to count all its practitioners, scattered around the world, practicing in their own homes to DVDs, moving slowly in parks and on beaches, and working alone with personal trainers?

We might also say that tai chi is in fact not a martial art itself but simply a sub-form of kung fu, a larger category that includes a huge number of schools, including wing chun, bagua quan and a whole host of others. The word "kung fu" itself—"gong fu" in the modern pinyin Romanization system—simply refers to "skill." A capable wall plasterer can be considered to have good gong fu if he does his job well. That would certainly make kung fu the world's most practiced martial art!

Even if we restrict gong fu to wushu—literally "fighting skills"—then we're still left with the question of whether we should be counting all of the different forms separately or as one Chinese school. For kung fu practitioners, different fighting styles can be broken down into "families" (*jia*), "sects" (*pai*) and schools (*men*). These themselves can be sub-divided into northern and southern schools, and "internal" and "external" forms. And if these sound like subtle variations on the same theme, it is worth pointing out that the differences between the different kinds of martial art are important. The founder of bak mei, for example, has been accused of being a traitor from the Shaolin temple and it's believed that some kung fu teachers will refuse to train a martial artist who has previously learned that form.

If we were to say that kung fu is the world's most popular form of martial arts then, we would also need to ask which kind of kung fu we were talking about.

What we can say then is this. Kung fu has popularized martial arts. By creating a form rich in acrobatics and aesthetics, it was able to carve a niche for itself in entertainment stretching right back to the Yuan dynasty of the thirteenth and fourteenth centuries. It's been used in Chinese opera for centuries and the beauty of its moves have made it a staple of movies from Bruce Lee's kung fu films to *The Matrix* and other Hollywood blockbusters.

Kung fu may—or may not—be the most popular form of martial arts in terms of the number of its practitioners but it certainly has a special place in the hearts of both martial artists and the general public.

One the other hand, kung fu is not an Olympic sport and there's no question that an organized sporting infrastructure can certainly help to spread the popularity of a form of martial arts, even if it does also restrict its development and force it to follow set rules. Authors Park Yeon Hwan and Jon Gerrard have named tae kwon do as the world's most popular martial art and there's no question that its presence at the Olympic games has given it a profile that many other forms would envy.

The same though can be said of judo and karate.

Ultimately, there's no way of knowing for sure which form of martial arts has the most practitioners. But kung fu certainly has a special role in the development of martial arts and even the students of all its various forms don't outnumber students of judo, karate or tae kwon do, it's certainly among the most appreciated, admired and enjoyed—both by the people who practice it and the people who watch it.

MYTH **15**

TAI CHI IS NOT A MARTIAL ART

Martial arts usually involves quick movements. To beat an attacker in a fight, you'll need fast reactions, rapid steps and powerful blows. You'll have to spot opportunities, exploit weaknesses and get your attacks in before your opponent can even see what's happening. You'll want him on the floor before he has time to respond to your first block.

That's why most martial arts emphasize the constant practice of technique. When a series of moves becomes second nature, you don't have to waste time thinking about you're going to do or where you're going to hit next. When you've spent hours sparring in a gym, you learn to spot attacks developing right at the beginning and you prepare your blocks by instinct.

With time and practice, your moves and your reactions reach the kind of speed you'll need to defend yourself in a real fighting situation.

Tai chi practitioners though move slowly. Their movements are graceful and attractive but they don't even attempt to develop speed, power or urgency. Many of them, in fact, appear to have nothing at all to do with martial arts. They seem to be more about achieving harmony and improving health than learning self-defense. It's no wonder then that so many people—including many who practice tai chi—will argue that tai chi has nothing to do with martial arts.

Nothing could be further from the truth.

Tai chi has its origins in the same area of China as the Shaolin temple. The name, which can also be written "taijiquan," means "supreme ultimate fist" and while it sounds similar, it has nothing to do with qi, which in some Romanization systems can also be written "chi." Tai chi students do attempt to control their "life force" but it's not a part of the school's name.

The goals of tai chi can broken down into three areas: health; meditation; and martial arts. That regular training and slow movements can deliver the first two is clear but beyond the fact that tai chi's movements copy those of martial arts schools—they imitate blocking, striking and kicking—are they really martial arts when they're practiced in this way: as "internal" forms that are practiced slowly and for reasons other than pure self-defense?

Much depends on the type of tai chi you're looking at. Just as there are many different forms of kung fu, so there are five different types of tai chi: chen, yang, wu or wu hao, wu and sun. Of these, yang is the most popular and was created by Yang Lu-ch'an in the nineteenth century who was hired by the Chinese court to teach his form of tai chi to the Palace Battalion of the Imperial Guards.

Yang also taught tai chi to his sons one of whom, Yang Ch'eng-fu, removed the more explosive and sudden movements, turning this form of tai chi into the slow, gentle techniques practiced so widely today.

Chen, the oldest form of tai chi and said to date back to the seventeenth century however, places the greatest emphasis on tai chi as a martial art. It uses low stances and has retained the explosive bursts of power known as *"fa jin."* Chen tai chi even uses a number of different weapons forms, teaching moves that are supposed to be practiced with halberds, swords, staffs and combinations of different weapons.

The Chen family may also have been responsible for the development of "pushing hands" ("*tui shou*"), an exercise designed to help students understand leverage, timing, coordination and positioning among other essential fighting skills. As an attacker pushes, the sparring partner must use the "thirteen original movements of tai chi" to redirect or ward off the attack. It's the closest tai chi comes to practicing defensive and offensive combat moves in a sparring environment, and it has become a competitive sport.

It should be clear then that tai chi has its origins in martial arts. It can draw links back to the most influential source of Chinese combat training. Its moves are based on combat techniques and at least some tai chi forms retain the explosive power of those moves. Its sparring exercises are certainly intended to ward off attack even though their most offensive moves are limited to a stiff shove.

But can it pass what should really be the ultimate test of any martial art: would the moves practiced every morning by tai chi students around the world be of any use at all in a real combat situation?

According to Dr. Yang Jwing-Ming, a martial arts teacher for more than 35 years and the author of 25 books including *Tai Chi Chuan Martial Applications*, there's no question that tai chi can be used for self-defense. It has limitations: tai chi practitioners only spar by pushing hands, a very gently form of sparring; without the proper amount of care, tai chi experts can often find themselves out of position and even off-balance; and often, tai chi practitioners neglect the role of kicks in favor pushes and blows.

But if the connection is right, he argues, and more importantly if the timing is correct, then tai chi's moves contain all of the techniques anyone needs to defend themselves.

It's not that tai chi isn't a martial art then, it's that tai chi is rarely practiced as a martial art. Change the training, include free forms and free fighting in tai chi's training routines, and tai chi's potential to defend and counterattack should quickly become clear.

MYTH 16

IF A MARTIAL ARTS STYLE WAS REALLY EFFECTIVE, IT WOULD FORM A PART OF MILITARY TRAINING

A lot of claims are made about martial arts. Learn this technique, some teachers will say, and you'll be able to stop a knife attacker in his tracks, disarm him and walk even the toughest streets in confidence. Practice these methods and you'll be able to disable a thug with just a finger poke and a slap to the right spot, say others. Understand leverage and grappling like our students do, say more martial arts sensei, and you'll be able to handle yourself in any real street fight.

But martial arts teachers aren't the best judges of the effectiveness of their martial arts schools. They'll always think their own schools and their own methods are the best.

Nor is the popularity of a martial arts school a sign that it's the smartest choice for anyone worried that they might need to beat off an attacker. People often choose a martial arts school because it's the only type of combat skill being taught in the local community center. Marketing is as big a factor as martial knowledge.

But a country's armed forces are free to choose any method of training their soldiers they want, and they'll always choose the techniques that are going to be the most effective in a real combat situation. This isn't a question of teaching people who fear that they might, one day, get in the odd fight—but don't expect that to happen really and in the meantime are happy to learn a few fighting skills. Armed forces have a responsibility to give their soldiers the skills they need to survive real hand-to-hand fights, the kind where failure means death and not just a stolen wallet or a loss of face.

If martial arts were really effective then, armed forces would be teaching them.

And they do.

In fact, they always have done. Many martial arts forms have their origins in the training techniques of professional armies. The core of kalarippayattu, for example, the ancient Indian martial art form, involves fighting with a sword and shield. Fencing too clearly has its source in European military training methods.

While some martial arts then have flowed from the army into civilian life, at least as much martial arts knowledge has moved from civilians into the military.

Shaolin monks are probably the most obvious example of this knowledge-sharing. According to legend, staff-fighting skills first reached the temple when the monk Bodhidarma stayed at the temple long enough to fight off an attack from bandits. But as we've seen, as early as the seventh century, Shaolin's monks were incorporated into the imperial army after helping a rebel leader to seize the throne, and one monk was even made General-in-Chief.

It's hard to believe that with a Shaolin monk at the head of the armed forces, that Chinese soldiers weren't learning at least some of the elements of Shaolin kung fu.

But it's not just the ancients who have seen the value of incorporating martial arts into military training. (Alexander the Great too made sure that his soldiers knew how to wrestle like pankration champions).

Sambo, a Russian self-defense system, comes in five different forms. Sport sambo is very similar to judo, as is freestyle sambo, an American version which allows choke holds and submissions, and was created to attract judokas. But self-defense sambo is an offshoot of combat sambo, which was developed for and used by the Russian military. It includes weapons and disarming techniques but it's also practiced as a competitive sport. Special sambo, on the other hand, was created to be used by special forces and Rapid React Police. The particular moves it emphasizes vary from unit to unit, but it's all based on the same combined martial arts form that includes both standing attacks and floor-based grappling.

Sambo was developed specifically for Russia's modern military, even if it did draw on wrestling techniques—including judo— that have been around for centuries. The Israeli army's krav maga training however was originally designed by former wrestler and boxer Imi Lichtenfield, who had created it in the 1930s to help the Jewish community to protect itself against Nazi attacks. When Israel declared independence, Lichtenfield was named Chief Instructor of Physical Fitness, and today the techniques still make up part of the Israel Defense Force's basic training. It's also used by the Israeli police as well as by the armed forces of many other countries, including Sweden.

The spread of krav maga around the world—it's said to be the world's fastest-growing martial arts form—might suggest that its techniques must then be the most effective for the kinds of situation that soldiers might face. But tae kwon do is a part of South Korean basic training and their soldiers are likely to face situations as dangerous as soldiers anywhere else.

In general then, we can see that martial arts knowledge has been taken up by armed forces and then spread beyond the military, and it's also been adopted by armies keen to give their soldiers the best-known fighting techniques.

Usually, those techniques taught in military courses tend to be comprehensive, covering strikes and kicks but also the kind of grappling and wrestling that many real fights descend towards.

But none of that means that any of the forms used by armies are going to be right for you. Unless you're a soldier, you'll want to choose a martial arts form that meets your specific needs, whether that's purely self-defense or something that includes plenty of history, tradition and physical challenge too.

MYTH **17**

GIRLS CAN'T AND SHOULDN'T DO MARTIAL ARTS

You'd have thought that Buffy would have killed off this myth. Years of high-kicking vampires, demons and other assorted bad guys into oblivion should have frightened anyone away from claiming that girls can't and shouldn't practice martial arts.

And yet the idea persists.

Mostly it comes from boys concerned about being beaten up by a girl. That's just something they'll have to get used to. Whenever you take up martial arts, you have to accept that you're going to get beaten. There's no shame in that while you're learning—it's how you learn—and there's certainly no shame in being floored by a girl who's been learning longer than you, does it better than you and is a more skilled fighter than you.

Some of the criticism comes from people who believe that girls shouldn't do such nasty things as learning how to kick someone in the head or deliver an elbow to their nose. They should be learning embroidery, knitting or soufflé-making. That's not just a strange idea about what it means to be a girl, it's also dangerous. Girls face special risks and their need to learn how to defend themselves is even more urgent than that of boys. And even if they don't feel threatened, no one should be telling girls what they should and shouldn't be doing.

If a girl wants to learn how to kickbox instead of scrapbook, there are no good reasons for standing in her way—and once she's been training for a while, plenty of good reasons not to.

And even the appropriateness of girls and boys grappling together on judo mats has been dealt with. Just because girls and boys do the same sport and the same martial art doesn't mean that they have to do them together or spar together. Martial arts that are practiced at a distance or with little contact, such as certain types of kung fu or tai chi can certainly be practiced in mixed classes. Other types, such as tae kwon do or sambo might be better studied in single-sex classes.

It's not just false that girls shouldn't be learning martial arts though. It's also wrong to say that they *can't* learn martial arts, that they're not as capable or as skilled as boys.

That's also nonsense.

Experienced instructors who have trained both boys and girls often find that girls are actually better students at least until about the age of puberty when boys begin to take the classes a bit more seriously. Some of that is down to behavior. Boys who take up martial arts are often attracted by the machismo that comes from believing that they can beat people up. They're less likely to follow instruction and more likely to goof around than put effort into practicing their moves.

Girls are often more willing to learn and less likely to believe that they know it all already.

Strength is not always a factor either. Size, weight and sheer physical power can be an important part of some martial arts, but that's true among boys too. Weight classes help to even the field and make competition meaningful. A slim 16-year-old girl with a black belt in judo might struggle to bring down a male heavyweight champion of the same martial art, but she'd do fine among her peers and could certainly beat many untrained men too.

And often, girls have an advantage when it comes to learning martial arts that goes beyond their willingness to learn. While strength might be important, flexibility, reflexes and endurance are even more important in many forms of martial arts.

That's not true for all forms, of course. Female kickboxers have to learn how to deliver their blows with force. But for tai chi, tae kwon do and many other forms, control, balance and precision are far more vital than power. With the right leverage, after all, it's possible to move even the heaviest object, and movement and momentum are the principles behind many martial arts techniques.

All of this should explain why not only are girls capable of learning martial arts, they've also been doing it for a very long time.

According to one Chinese story, after the Manchu empire conquered China and replaced the Ming dynasty with its own Qing rule, it faced a threat from Shaolin monks loyal to the old regime. The Imperial army conquered the temple, killing many of the monks. Five monks however, were able to escape, include the nun Ng Moy who fled to the White Crane Temple in the south.

One day, Ng Moy noticed a cat attacking a crane. The crane didn't run and it didn't panic. It remained calm and was able to fend off the attacks until the cat grew tired and gave up. Ng Moy adapted what she saw to her own Shaolin training to create a new form of martial art.

Near the temple lived a young woman called Yim Wing Chun and her father Yim Yee. Wing Chun was engaged to Leung Bok Chau but she was being pestered by the leader of a local gang who wanted to marry her himself. Ng Moy taught Wing Chun her new martial art, and suggested that her father tell the gang leader that Wing Chun would marry him but only if he was able to beat her in combat.

Not only did Wing Chun beat the gang leader, she beat up his gang too—and married her fiancé. When Wing Chun asked Ng Moy the name of the type of kung fu she had learnt, Ng Moy named it after her.

The story, of course, might not be true but if Bruce Lee had no problem learning a martial art that is said to have been created by a woman, no one should object to girls practicing martial arts.

MYTH 18

MARTIAL ARTS IS ONLY FOR THE YOUNG

Martial arts novels can sometimes leave the impression that training in unarmed combat was created by senior citizens to improve the well-being and self-esteem of old people. Again and again we find descriptions of apparently feeble old men who, when faced with a gang of bad guys, reveal that their walking sticks are secret weapons and their feet—despite the arthritis—are capable of reaching the chins of two bullies with one kick.

And yet, step into most martial arts gyms and you'll find very few 60-year-olds sparring on the floor or practicing with a punch bag. Instead, you'll often find small children practicing moves they barely understand, teenagers looking to boost their confidence with knowledge of how to defend themselves, and perhaps just a handful of senior citizens curious to learn about martial arts and keen to study its secrets.

Martial arts stories might be filled with examples of grey-haired men battling gang members half their age but in real life, too many seem to believe that the training is only for the young.

Part of the reason may lie in the West's view of martial arts as a kind of sport, a way of staying in shape, keeping fit and being physically active. It's a pastime that's supposed to ensure that old age is healthy, not something to be considered once you've reached that age. Just as pensioners tend not to throw footballs or run bases so kicks and jumps are best left to those with supple joints and strong bones.

To some extent, all of that is true. Some types of martial arts can be too physically demanding for the very old to practice all of the techniques. But on the whole, martial arts is ideal for any age and delivers different benefits to different age groups.

For very small children, including those aged as young as 3 or 4, martial arts training clearly has little to do with self-defense or spirituality. It's a fun exercise, a way to move around, release energy in a safe environment and perhaps enable a coach to identify potential in a particularly gifted child. The children though have to be capable of standing still, following instructions and copying what they're taught.

For slightly older children, often the starting point for many practitioners, martial arts can be a useful after-school activity that as well as teaching self-defense also enables children to learn discipline, raise their confidence and stay fit and in shape. Although many of these children may give up martial arts as they grow older, those early lessons will remain with them. Others will continue practicing and training, benefitting from a lifetime of discipline and learning.

And for teenagers, martial arts also delivers an understanding of responsibility and self-control. Having been taught to harm others, they must also learn the limits of their power and the right—and wrong times—to use it. For young people entering adulthood, martial arts training can represent all of the most important issues that they'll face in the years ahead.

But older practitioners bring a number of advantages to training that can benefit both themselves and other martial artists.

Their maturity in particular gives them a focus and a patience that are essential for learning the nuances of different moves, understanding how and why they work, and practicing them until they feel natural. While young martial artists often want to head straight to the most powerful offensive moves, older students tend to be happy to master one move at a time, and they're less interested in developing the potential to harm an opponent than in the satisfaction of a move well-executed.

Their discipline, curiosity and willingness to learn make them among the keenest students and often the best learners.

That makes them useful additions to the class but of course, learning martial arts also brings wonderful health benefits for the older students themselves.

In China, this is understood. Parks in China, Taiwan and other parts of Asia fill in the early morning and evening with retirees gracefully swinging their arms and practicing their slow kicks as a way of moving their qi. Often they can even be found doing more energetic exercises, including dangling from tree branches and practicing stretches. Tai chi, a form particularly popular with pensioners, might have the appearance of a physical meditation but its moves are based on genuine martial arts techniques which, practiced at real speed, can be highly effective. As we've seen, the form itself comes from the same area as the Shaolin temple.

According to Dr. Benjamin Kligler, medical director of New York's New Beth Israel Center for Health and Healing, practicing tai chi can lower stress levels, curing recurrent headaches, stomach reflux and other anxiety-related problems. Because it's low-impact, it can also lubricate the joints and help strengthen bones in osteoporosis sufferers.

Each martial arts school offers different benefits, different challenges and makes different demands on its practitioners. While the young can certainly benefit from practicing martial arts then, exactly the same is true for older practitioners who can also find a form that meet their needs and delivers real benefits as well as self-defense awareness.

Martial arts isn't just suitable for the young; practiced with care, it's good for everyone.

MYTH **19**

SIZE AND STRENGTH ARE IRRELEVANT IN MARTIAL ARTS

One of the promises that some martial arts instructors use to persuade students to join their classes is that with the right training, they'll be able to beat off any attacker. It doesn't matter how big the person wielding the knife might be. It doesn't matter how much they've worked out or whether their shirt is hiding rippling muscles or skin and bone. With the right techniques and an understand of martial arts, even a 60-pound girl will have them flying through the air and begging for mercy.

To some extent, that's true.

There are many martial arts forms for which strength and size are completely irrelevant. The pushing hands techniques used in tai chi, for example, rely precisely on the power of the attacker. The more he pushes, the greater the effect when the defender gives way. The stronger the attacker, the more momentum he has, and the faster he'll fall.

But pushing hands is not the same as fighting. The techniques could help to develop moves that might help someone to defend themselves against attack but the sparring itself relies on the willingness of the attacker to push only with his hands, and not with the full weight of his body—as is likely to happen in a real fight. Pushing hands is a training exercise designed to develop skill in martial arts, as well as calmness and confidence. It's not a self-defense regime alone.

For many martial arts in fact, weight and strength are so important a factor in determining who would win a fight that their competitions are organized into different classes. Tae kwon do has sixteen weight classes and judo, which uses locks and throws rather than the brute power of kicks and punches, has eight. According to Emilio Bruno though, a key figure in the modern development of judo, when weight classes were first introduced to the sport, there were only four divisions, including one called "unlimited," in which skill would be the only factor. In a letter to wrestling historian Don Sayenga, he wrote:

> *To preserve the "little man versus the big man" theory, the Grand Championships were established where the weight system was eliminated and the skills of true judo can further exemplify the principle of "Maximum Efficiency with Minimum of Effort", Dr. Kano's established "All Pervading Principle of Judo."*

While that suggests that a light but skilled judoka should be able to overcome a more powerful judoka, it doesn't seem to have happened often enough for the weight classes to have been abolished. Instead, they grew.

Nor were judo and tae kwon do alone in recognizing that while skill is certainly important, the amount of power that a martial artist brings to a fight can affect his chances of winning.

Perhaps the most important example of this is Bruce Lee's own commitment to bodybuilding.

When Bruce Lee moved away from wing chun to create a more effective and comprehensive form of martial art in jeet kune do, he noted that too much time was given to training in technique and too little time to training the individual. He used weights to build up his own muscle mass particularly his arms and abdominal muscles.

His daily two-hour workout consisted of bicep curls, squats, push-ups, reverse curls and skipping rope. He would later spend another hour each day weight training and cycling.

Despite being a kung fu martial artist who never took part in a professional competition, his understanding of the importance of strength meant that he had the training schedule of a professional boxer and the physique of a bodybuilder.

And for good reason.

According to Martina Sprague, martial artist, historian and author of *Strength and Power Training for Martial Arts*, strength training is a vital part of preparation for just about any martial art.

Technique, she says, is important, and a good understand of moves, together with intelligence and courage can help a smaller or weaker adversary defeat a stronger attacker. But strength also increases confidence and raises the pain threshold, allowing the defender to absorb and survive heavy blows.

While it's true that lifting weights alone will not make someone a better martial artist—only skills training can do that—it can make someone into a stronger martial artist. That means their punches will land harder, their kicks will be more powerful, and their blocks will be firmer. Nor will those larger muscles have any negative effect on flexibility or speed.

Most importantly, that extra bulk might well have the ultimate effect on a would-be attacker: it could deter them from attacking in the first place.

Strength and size will always be a factor in a real fight. That's why so many martial arts have weight classes and why so many leading martial arts masters have put such efforts into bodybuilding.

But not all martial arts students learn their techniques in order to compete against other fighters with the same techniques. Many do it because they want to defend themselves. For those students, size matters far less, and more important will be the skills that allow them to strike and floor an untrained opponent—and the courage to use them.

MYTH **20**

TO DO MARTIAL ARTS, YOU HAVE TO ENJOY PHYSICAL COMBAT

One of the great benefits of teaching martial arts is that you get to meet such a wide range of different kinds of people. A typical martial arts class will have students looking to improve their fitness. There will be enthusiasts keen to learn everything there is to know about the form of martial arts you teach. There will be talented fighters who can master even the most complex of moves in a flash, and there will be people who will always struggle but who will keep coming back because they love learning.

And there will always be one or two people who have taken up martial arts simply because they like hitting people.

They can't do that in real life because they'll be arrested so they've chosen to take up a hobby which will allow them to work off their aggression and smack some people about in a legitimate, legal setting.

You can always tell who they are because they're the worst martial artists in the room. They don't bother to learn the blocks properly. They don't have the patience to practice technique until the moves are smooth and perfect. And when they lash out, they put all of their focus into power instead of finesse and accuracy. When people choose to take up martial arts because they enjoy physical combat, the result is often poor martial arts and an experience that's not fun for them or their sparring partner.

Martial arts *is* a physical sport. There is a real sense of pleasure in learning a new move and performing it exactly the way it should be performed. Whether you're practicing a new karate kata, exploring a judo throw, or breaking in a new tae kwon do technique, understanding how it works, delivering it correctly and seeing the results—whether that's contact exactly where you wanted to make contact or a successful throw—should be fun.

But that's not the same as enjoying physical combat. That's enjoying a physical challenge.

It's getting a kick out of learning something new, pushing your body as far as it can go and feeling that you're in touch with a tradition that might well go back hundreds and even thousands of years.

That might be why in a typical martial arts class, the numbers of people who really don't like physical combat usually outnumber the people who do. In one online poll of 777 martial artists, 24 percent of respondents said that they had taken up martial arts "to better defend myself from attack." A further 19 percent had done it "to improve my fitness."

Only 3 percent confessed that they practiced martial arts because "I like to hurt others."

People who take up martial arts for self-defense or for physical fitness aren't doing it because they enjoy physical combat. On the contrary, if you're looking to defend yourself, it's because you don't want to take part in fights. You want to make sure that any fight you do find yourself caught up in ends quickly and with you on the winning side.

And while martial arts training can certainly make someone fit, taking part in a lot of fights is more likely to lead at some point to physical injury than to the peak of physical fitness. Training makes for a good workout but fighting is far from healthy. Even the best fighters get hurt sometimes.

So an enjoyment of physical combat isn't just unnecessary for martial arts, it can actually get in the way of many of the goals that people who take up martial arts want to reach.

In fact, it's even possible to practice martial arts without any desire to engage in any form of physical combat at all.

Tai chi is the most obvious example of this. Although the moves practiced during tai chi are based on combat forms—and, as we've seen, can be used in combat—not all forms of tai chi involve sparring. Fighting skills are often far less important to tai chi practitioners than meditation, relaxation and harmony.

But perhaps the best example of a martial arts in which physical combat plays little—if any—part is boabom.

An ancient Tibetan martial art, boabom is focused almost entirely on health. Its movements are said to be "related to channels and nets of energy that, when animated in conjunction with one another and with a positive mind, can awaken an uncommon internal force and an ascending cycle of strengthening health," as one writer puts it. Osseous Boabom, one of the three boabom forms, is often called the "art of self-medicine through self-defense." The principles of the boabom school include causing no harm to the body so there's no contact at all. Nor is there any competition or belts. Classes are meant to be relaxed, calm places in which no one hits, kicks or throws anyone and everyone leaves feeling better than they came in.

There's nothing about the pleasures of physical combat.

None of this means that people who enjoy physical combat shouldn't take up martial arts. There are plenty of full-contact martial arts forms that might well benefit people who do enjoy the fights.

But you don't have to enjoy physical combat to get the most out of martial arts.

MYTH **21**

TO DEVELOP THE STRENGTH FOR MARTIAL ARTS, YOU HAVE TO WORK OUT AND CONSUME VAST QUANTITIES OF PROTEIN

This is a myth that's partially true. Martial arts is a sport. It doesn't always look like one. Not all forms are competitive so there aren't always winners and losers. A great deal of emphasis is placed on technique and practice, rather than physical training and fitness. And the constant learning of new moves and the passing of exams to win new belt grades can make martial arts feel more like an after-school studying activity than a physical pastime.

If you have to study and take tests, it can't have anything to do with sport, can it? It must be school.

In fact, of course, martial arts is certainly physical and while the tests required to move up a dan level will examine knowledge and skill, the biggest test in martial arts is a physical one. To practice most martial arts well, you will need to do at least some form of physical training.

The kind of training you have to do though depends on the martial art and it rarely requires the kind of vast protein consumption practiced by bodybuilders and other athletes.

Most martial arts make three physical demands.

The first is for flexibility.

This is true of just about every kind of martial art from the most internal form of tai chi to the most violent combination of mixed martial arts. A tai chi student must be able to move freely through the different combination of moves just as a sambo fighter must have the ability to grapple with an opponent on the ground, escape locks and apply chokes.

The exercises required to improve flexibility though have nothing to do with endless protein shakes and giant plates of pasta. According to Sang H. Kim, a martial arts teacher and author of *Ultimate Flexibility: A Complete Guide to Stretching for Martial Arts*, it's possible to achieve the required level of flexibility in all of the main muscle groups with no more than fifteen minutes of exercise a day. A typical exercise might involve standing with your back to a chair and about three feet away from it. Place your hands on the back of the chair and bend your knees and elbows until you are in a sitting position.

Exercises like these help to stretch the shoulders, chest and upper arms, and are important for striking, grappling and weapons techniques.

But none of them involve going for the burn or breaking into a serious sweat.

The same is true of speed.

There are plenty of martial arts stories about fighters who can land twenty blows before the opponent can manage to say "Please stop hitting me." The stories of Bruce Lee's unbeatable speed and reflexes have generated almost as many legends as there are martial arts novels. And movies make much of the whooshing sound that fists make as they fly through the air at high speed towards their target. (Even though in real life, of course, they don't make any sound except a horrible crunch on impact.)

In practice, that sort of speed is both unrealistic and undesirable. You'd be much better off landing one knockout blow on an opponent—a punch packed with force and power, and delivered to the right spot—than trying to land multiple, repeated but light blows.

But there is still an advantage in being able to respond quickly to attacks, react fast to get in the block then return the punch or kick at a speed high enough to unbalance your opponent.

One exercise, described in J.Barnes' guide *Speed Training for Martial Arts: How to Maximize Speed for Competition and Self-Defense*, involves holding a book about six inches in front of your face. Allow the book to fall then deliver a punch and pull back your fist fast enough to catch the book before it hits the floor.

Again, it's easy to see how developing that sort of speed can improve martial arts techniques. But it's just as easy to see that exercises like these don't require lifting large amounts of weights or loading up on bulk.

But strength is important and you will need strong muscles to learn martial arts. With high muscular endurance, you'll be able to absorb blows better; you'll be more relaxed during sparring and fighting; and you'll be able to cope better with the physical challenges involved in training.

The abdomen is particularly important, an area that Bruce Lee emphasized in his own workouts. Weak abdominal muscles are likely to cause lower back strains and lead to weak kicks. It's why many instructors focus first on stances, steps and punches while the students get in shape for the kicks.

And as we've seen, big muscles are also likely to put off big bullies, meaning that you'll never actually have to use the martial arts techniques you'll be learning.

So while it's not necessary to do massive amounts of weightlifting and protein guzzling to be a martial artist, you should be looking for ways to get in shape. You want to be strong as well as flexible, fast and knowledgeable.

MYTH **22**

MARTIAL ARTS REQUIRES ALL SORTS OF BIZARRE AND EXPENSIVE EQUIPMENT

Sports equipment is big business. In 2008, sales of sports gear reached over $69 billion worldwide—and that doesn't include clothes, snowmobiles or new Nike shoes that seem to cost several million dollars a pair. More than a fifth of that money went on golf equipment but it's safe to say that a large chunk went on martial arts gear too. Certainly, catalogs are stuffed with all sorts of fighting equipment from shorts and belts to swords and sharp-pointed throwing stars.

Some of that equipment looks pretty strange. The weapons section of any martial arts store could well offer *nunchaku* (split poles connected by short chains), *kamas* (sickle-like tools that look like they've been swiped off a mini Grim Reaper), *sai*, (a long, stiletto sword with a wavy hand guard) and so many different kinds of sticks, swords and other assorted killing tools, you'll wonder where the average martial arts expert puts it all.

The answer, of course, is that he doesn't. These weapons might be called "martial arts weapons," and it's possible that some of them (although not all of them) may have once formed part of the training at a traditional kung fu school or samurai training center, but it's unlikely that you'll ever be taught how to use them in a martial arts class.

And for good reason.

Few people walk around with nunchaku in their bags so when it comes to self defense, they have to know how to use the most important fighting tools that they'll always have at their disposal: their arms and legs. Even learning how to fight with a staff—once the specialty of the Shaolin temple—is these days ignored in favor of knowing how to deliver punches and kicks, or poke an attacker quickly in the eye.

Unless you're learning fencing, archery or kendo—or unless you're studying interior design for martial arts schools—you should be able to leave all of the strange, expensive and dangerous-looking weapons far behind.

But it's not just all of those different killing tools that martial arts stores will insist you consider buying. Most of the things in the store actually intended to protect you from being hurt. Take up tae kwon do, for example, and your list of must-have protective gear will include: a head guard; a groin guard; a chest protector; forearm pads; shin pads; a mouth guard; tae kwon do boots; and gloves.

Many of those things are both sensible and necessary. Tae kwon do involves high kicks to the head and while part of your training will include trying to block those attacks, you can expect a few of them to get through. Unless you're prepared to be knocked out several times a week, you will need something to absorb the blows—and schools linked to both the World Taekwondo Federation and the International Taekwondo Federation require that students wear them before sparring.

Forearm and shin pads help to prevent bruising while blocking blows, a mouth guard ensures that you don't lose your teeth when your blocks don't work, and as for groin guards… well, if a guy doesn't want to wear one, then he might find that he does well one day in the women's competition.

Each of those items could cost you between $20 and $30 so you could easily find yourself paying out as much $150 for a complete set of the gear you'll need to take up tae kwon do seriously. Other martial arts—especially those that do sparring—have similar requirements.

But in practice, you should find that most martial arts schools will make no demands at all at the beginning. They'll supply the punch bags and targets that you can punch and kick, and they might even have a few spare sets of protective gear that you can use until you get your own. And when you do decide that martial arts is for you and that it's worth making the investment, there are often ways to pick up all the gear you need relatively cheaply.

The school itself might be able to supply the gear. Larger schools often buy equipment in bulk, winning a discount that they can pass on to their students. It's also worth looking at notice boards at the school. As students move on they'll be looking to leave their old equipment behind. Some of that gear you can also find on eBay.

If you're really keen to save a few bucks, Michael D. Janich's book *Homemade Martial Arts Training Equipment: A Do-It-Yourself Guide* will teach you how to make target pads, punch bags, abdominal exercisers and a whole range of other things from items that include empty soda bottles and old tires. You won't be the coolest kid in the dojo but you will be the thriftiest.

You only need this gear though if you're going to spar and not all martial arts do that. Internal martial arts forms, for example, and those that practice pushing hands won't require you to bring anything more unusual than comfortable clothes. You might not even need a uniform.

Ultimately, the amount you spend on equipment depends on you, on the type of martial art you want to learn and on how much you want to invest in it.

As you move forward with your martial arts training, you might consider it worthwhile laying out a few dollars on the sort of protective gear that will stop you going home looking like you just got hit by a bus. But to get started it's unlikely that you'll need anything more expensive or more bizarre than an enthusiasm to learn how to fight.

MYTH **23**

SOME MARTIAL ARTS MOVES ARE SO DANGEROUS THAT NO STYLE WILL TEACH THEM

It's a cliché that seems to run right through martial arts. Teachers will tell you the basic moves. They'll explain how to do blocks, deliver punches and kick higher than a pole dancer but they won't tell you the really serious stuff. They won't explain the simple triple-combination finger poke which, when delivered in the right place, delivers instant death.

Nor will they reveal the twelve sensitive spots on the human body which result in agonizing paralysis whenever a blow, struck at a certain speed and at a particular angle, hits them.

Nor will they even admit such lethal moves exist.

It's all done for a good reason, of course. If these moves become common knowledge then no one would ever be safe. Thugs would be going up to people in bars, poking them in the back and leaving them writhing on the floor in agony. Fully trained martial artists would cross to the dark side where they would become unstoppable enemies, constantly torturing, maiming and killing people.

Or perhaps just a touch more realistically, instead of using martial arts to avoid fights and employing the minimal amount of force necessary to win the battle, martial artists who knew the most lethal moves would be killing and disabling attackers who could have been stopped with much less dangerous methods.

Or even worse still, inexperienced students, uncertain of their technique and unaware of their own strengths, would end up using the most dangerous moves on their sparring partners and classmates. Instead of staying safe by learning martial arts, students could find that taking up martial arts becomes the most dangerous thing they've ever done.

And instructors will find themselves having to explain why their dojo keeps producing dead people instead of well-taught martial arts students.

If martial arts instructors choose to ditch the most dangerous moves from their teaching routines, who can blame them?

But they don't.

Martial arts is a dangerous activity and both students and instructors recognize that. It's even part of the attraction.

Martial arts students understand that they're going to learn how to hurt people. They'll learn how to cause them temporary damage in the form of the mild concussion felt by a solid kick to the head. They'll learn how to cause medium damage in the form of broken limbs and dislocated joints. They'll learn how to cause permanent damage in the form of gouged eyes and broken eardrums.

And they'll learn how to kill too.

There are all sorts of ways to do all of those things and during the lessons, students will learn many of them.

It's unlikely, of course, that any student will ever learn all of the most dangerous moves if only because different branches of martial arts know how to do different things.

A student of sambo, which is primarily a military-style martial arts, might learn how to choke an enemy soldier if they're forced to take them on hand-to-hand. They'll learn how to continue the hold well beyond stopping an attacker in his tracks, and even beyond disabling him.

They'll learn how to choke him to death.

A kung fu student too might be told about the most lethal vital points to deliver a kick or land a punch on. He'll learn what could happen if he gets his move exactly right and his opponent fails to block the attack. He'll be told just how dangerous those moves are—and he'll still be taught how to deliver them.

The instructor will explain the theory, describe what to do, and might even demonstrate the moves on a volunteer... up to a point.

But he won't show a fatal technique all the way through to its conclusion or allow his students to practice it, and for obvious reasons.

Martial arts clearly has some very lethal moves. It's supposed to have lethal moves. Those moves advanced, they're dangerous and they're not necessary for the average martial arts student who only wants to understand what his chosen form is about and defend himself in a fight if necessary.

But that doesn't mean that those moves aren't taught and explained.

There is no agreement across martial arts schools not to practice the most lethal moves. There is just the common sense of teachers who attempt to give the students knowledge about them without actually requiring them to use them in practice sessions.

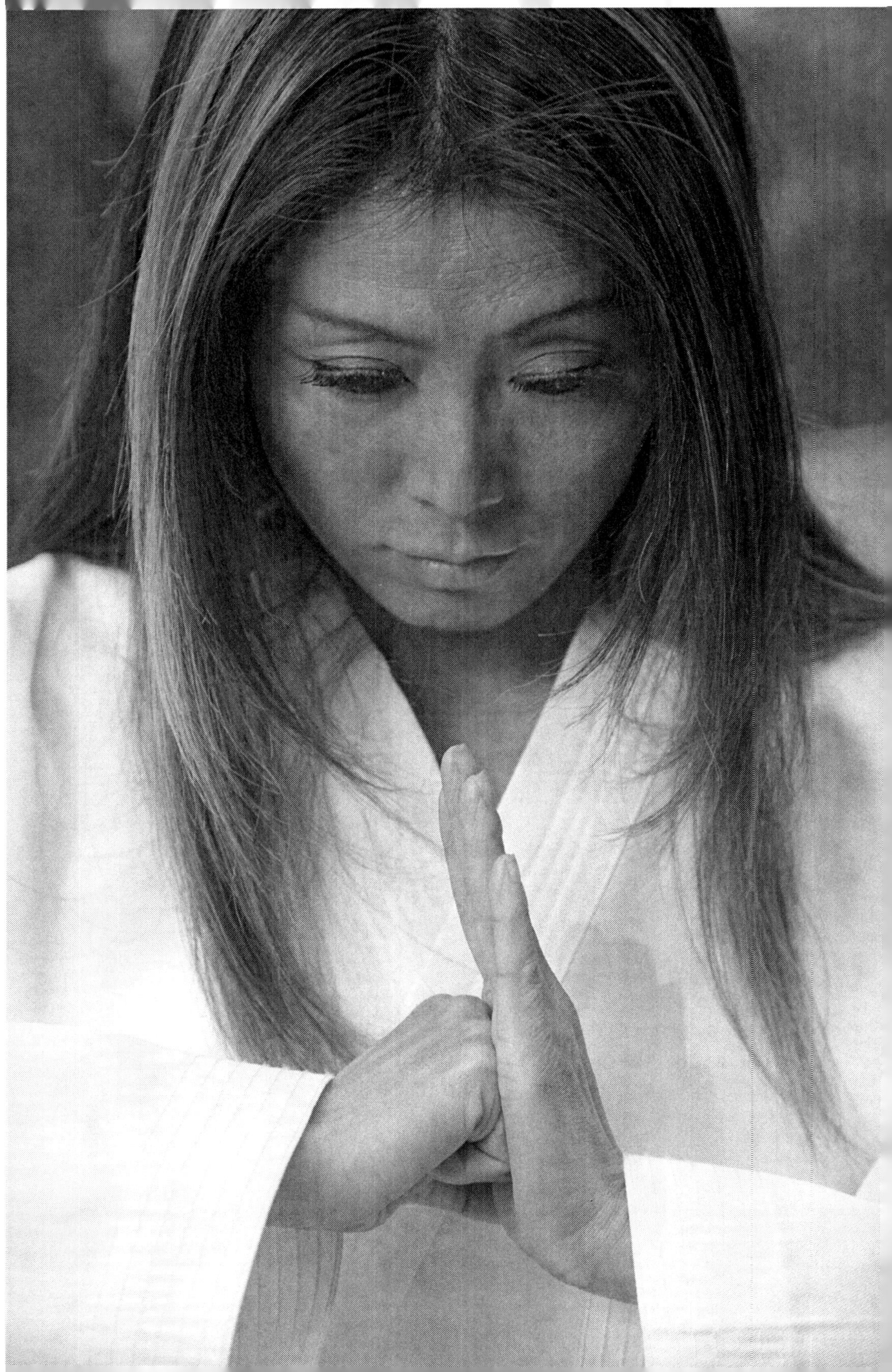

MYTH **24**

TO FIGHT EFFECTIVELY, YOU HAVE TO CHANNEL YOUR QI

Real fights tend be pretty quick affairs. There will be a look, an exchange of insults, an invasion of personal space, then before you know it, some pushing and shoving, a clumsily delivered blow or two and a group of friends pulling away the winner before he can be arrested for murder.

Martial arts fights—at least in the movies—tend to look rather different. The two parties will size each other up from a healthy distance. They'll strike their poses, then at some point they'll close their eyes and seem to start meditating.

What they're actually doing is gathering their qi, the life energy that is said to flow through all living things. It's an important part of eastern martial arts and the main element of the internal forms such as tai chi and ba gua quan. A fighter who can master his qi, it is believed, will enjoy better focus, greater balance and more powerful blows. Believe some of the articles in the more bizarre martial arts magazines and you could even end up convinced that with the correct control of qi, it's possible to repel attackers without even touching them, start fires without matches and deliver killing blows with a flick of your finger.

It's the kind of thing that makes for great martial arts movies but not very effective martial arts moves.

It might however, make for good medicine. Acupuncture, once included in the training of some martial arts forms, attempts to remove blockages in the body's flow of qi and much of Chinese medicine is devoted to creating a balanced flow of energy. It's the main goal for many of the people who practice qi gong.

Qi may also have another meaning in martial arts though. In addition to being a kind of energy that flows constantly through the body, qi can also refer to efficient fighting. When your body is correctly aligned, when you can perform your moves flawlessly and when everything just seems to slot into place, you might be said to have "proper qi." A more familiar way of putting it would be to say that you're "in the zone."

Qi is usually associated with internal forms of martial arts, and especially qi gong, which literally means "the skill of qi." But the distinction between internal and external martial arts forms is relatively new and was first made only about a hundred years ago. In practice, most Chinese martial arts forms will include elements of internal and external strength training, even if the emphases are different.

But qi isn't limited to Chinese martial arts forms. It isn't even limited to forms derived from China such as aikido and karate, both of which use qi in one way or another.

Indian martial artists also attempt to develop *sakti*, a power that can only be achieved through meditation. By focusing the mind in this way, fighters can remove fear, doubt and anxiety, all of which can cause hesitation and inhibit action during combat. While qi gong practitioners are likely to control their qi in silence, students of kalarippayattu are more likely to chant during their meditations.

And training in northern style kalarippayattu in particular also includes lessons on massage and ayurvedic medicine, both of which are necessary for an understanding of *prana*, an idea very similar to qi.

Silat, a Malay martial art practiced across Southeast Asia, has a similar concept too. According to silat practitioners, bodies are made up of energy circles called *chakra*. Energy that rotates outwards from the body and along diagonal lines is defensive. Energy that moves inwards is offensive. When a fighter understands his energy flows, he can match them to his movements, increasing the power of his attacks. And like qi, an understanding of *chakra* can also help pesilat—silat fighters—to manipulate pressure points both for healing and combat, and may even allow them to harm an attacker without touching them.

It may seem then that to learn martial arts, you first have to spend a great deal of time looking at maps of qi meridians, learning how to meditate and trying to focus your qi when you'd really rather be learning how to kick a mugger in the head before he can stab you.

In the West at least, that's rarely the case.

Martial arts practitioners who are attracted by the idea of mastering qi and enjoying the sense of relaxation and harmony that comes with it are likely to be drawn towards a qi gong or tai chi class. There, they will spend time moving quietly and slowly, and trying to get in touch with their body's energy flows.

Students who come to learn more external martial arts forms such as tae kwon do or judo are unlikely to spend a great deal of time—if any at all—learning about qi.

They might be taught how to collect their thoughts and stay calm in a fight. They could learn about the most important places to deliver blows or apply pressure. But they're not likely to learn about vital points and their ability to restrict the flow of qi in the same way that a student of kung fu might learn about them.

Qi is an important element of martial arts, and it's necessary for students of many forms to understand it. But there are plenty of schools too whose moves have nothing to do with qi and whose students won't have to channel anything but their passion for martial arts and their desire to learn and practice.

MYTH **25**

BREAKING BRICKS IS A SIGN OF ADVANCED MARTIAL ARTS SKILL

As a way of impressing an audience, it doesn't get much more dramatic. A martial artist walks up to pile of bricks, takes a deep breath and with a deafening shout chops straight through them with nothing but his bare hand. There's no bruise, no howl of agony and no way anyone is going to be anything but awestruck at the martial artist's skill and technique.

It's not a practice that's carried out by all forms of martial arts. Karatekas are perhaps the fighters best known for their ability to chop through almost anything that can be put in front of them, but it's likely that breaking actually originates with kung fu, and in particular with Iron Palm conditioning. Not a form of martial arts itself, Iron Palm is a series of exercises intended to enable fighters to strike hard without harming their hands.

Although different teachers will use different methods (and some of them are said to keep their own techniques secret), Iron Palm training usually has three elements.

The most important is conditioning. Students practice punching bags filled with coarse material such as gravel or stones to toughen up the skin and develop the tendons and ligaments. The principle is the same as that used by weightlifters: the more strain the body is placed under, the stronger it will be after it recovers. The hand is then treated with a liniment called dit da jow, which literally means "steel hit wine" to prevent bruising and help healing.

At the same time, students are taught how to strike hard. This usually involves relaxing the body, meditating in a standing position and releasing residual tension to pack a powerful blow.

Finally, fighters may also practice qi gong exercises to improve mental focus, ensure that all of their power is channeled into the point of impact and believe that they can break the objects without harming themselves.

Iron palm training can be fairly complex. Trainees need to remember to breathe out at the moment of impact. They try to relax as they strike rather than tense their arm and muscles, and they also practice with different parts of the hand, repeating the exercises daily.

Karatekas however, train by simply punching makiwara until it hurts too much. These are wooden posts fixed into the ground and wrapped with rope. Trainees strike the post with increasing power, giving themselves calluses and enlarged knuckles.

However the training is done though, it usually has a number of different goals beyond the ability to strike hard without breaking a hand or foot.

For some martial arts, for example, the ability to chop a pile of bricks with the bare hand is a test a trainee has to pass in order to move up a level.

There is some sense in that. Today it's possible to measure the power of a punch or a kick with an accelerometer. But there weren't any of those when these techniques were being developed so breaking bricks appeared to be a reasonable way of seeing just how powerful a blow a student could deliver.

Breaking performances though could also be put on for entertainment. Kung fu fighters have been appearing on the stage for hundreds of years longer than they've been appearing in movies. When smashing objects can look so impressive, breaking bricks would have been part of the performances used by temples and schools to raise money and attract students. That's still true today.

But does breaking bricks—and other objects—like this really mean that performer is a skilled martial artist?

Not necessarily. A board or a brick breaks for one of three reasons when the martial artist hits it.

It could be because of the speed of the blow. It could be because of the power behind the blow. Or it could be because of the kinetic energy of the blow. This last type of strike requires very little contact with the object, just enough to trigger a small shock wave that the causes the item to buckle and bend. If it's too brittle to buckle, it will break.

All of these strikes require a certain amount of technique. They all require skill and they all require training.

They're also pretty good signs that if the fighter lands a blow on an opponent, that blow is going to be strong and painful, but it's not going to harm the fighter at all.

But the power of a strike is only one aspect of martial arts, as is the ability to resist pain.

Breaking bricks shows that a martial artist has mastered some aspects of martial arts but it's no measure of how well they block attacks, put together multiple moves or maintain a balanced stance.

It certainly doesn't indicate how well they might do in a real fight.

Breaking bricks is difficult and dramatic but it's only one small part of any martial arts technique.

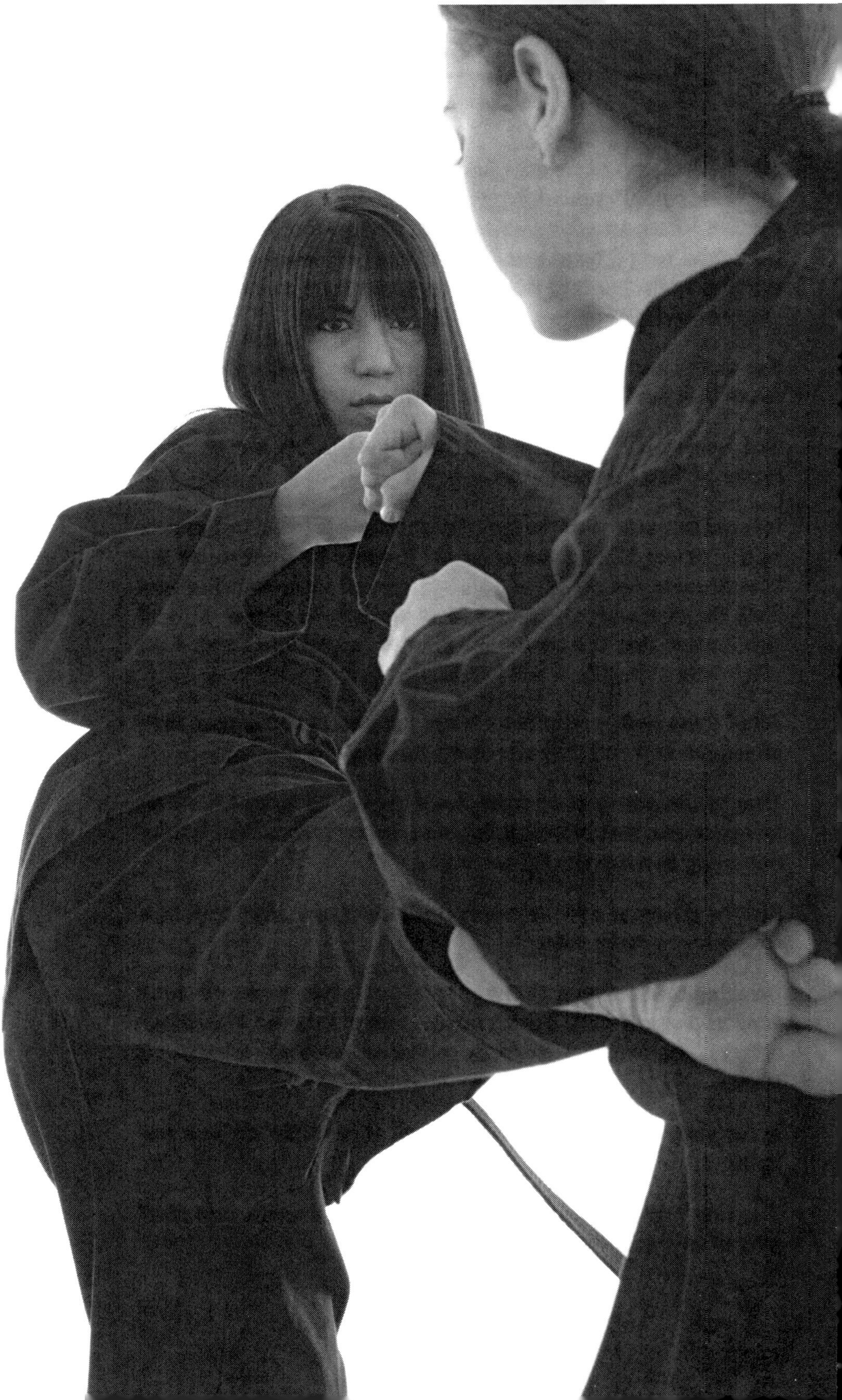

MYTH **26**

SOME FIGHTING TECHNIQUES ARE UNSTOPPABLE

Some martial artists like to believe that if they train long enough, if they reach the right level of technique and if they impress their sifu enough, he might just let them in on a little secret. He might tell them how to perform a move that no one can defend against.

It might not be the most dangerous move in the world. It might not be one that kill an opponent with one blow or cause them to lose control of their limbs. But it will be completely unstoppable and that's why it's been kept secret.

If everyone knew about it, then someone will have figured out a defense against it. Because it's been kept under wraps for centuries and only revealed to the best fighters in every school, that unstoppable move has remained unbeatable.

Most martial artists though don't believe a word of it. There are no secrets, they say, but there are moves which, if performed properly, can't be stopped by even the best martial artist. Defensive moves might be good enough to stop most attacks, they argue, but if these techniques are done well, they'll bust through any defense and always lay an opponent out cold.

Unfortunately, that's not true either.

There are thousands—probably tens of thousands—of different martial arts moves practiced across different types of martial arts around the world.

And for every move there is a defensive move that can stop it.

That doesn't mean that some moves aren't more powerful than others. Certainly, some techniques will always be harder to stop than others. But that's rarely because of the move itself, and more because of the fighter's ability to carry it out.

The chances that an attack will hit its target depend on speed and power. The faster an attack is made, the greater the chances that it will strike before the defender has a chance to put a block in place.

The greater the power behind the attack, the greater the ability of the attacker to push straight through a weak defense.

In tae kwon do, for example, the side kick and roundhouse kick are both believed to be among the most powerful of blows. But they're also among the most common, so tae kwon do fighters soon learn how to defend against them. Some fighters have responded then by delivering a high roundhouse kick that drops downwards at a 45 degree angle. It's hard to perform and just as hard to defend against. The weight of the leg alone is often enough to knock out any defense. But with the right position and good technique, it is stoppable.

Mark Mireles, a former marine, Los Angeles police officer and martial artist, has broken the moves hardest to defend against into three types. His book *Street Stoppers: The Martial Arts Most Devastating Trips, Sweeps and Throws for Real Fighting* argues that when it comes to taking opponents down—perhaps the most important achievement in winning a real fight—martial artists need to know how to trip, sweep and throw. The difference between them, he says, is that a trip strikes below the knee; a sweep takes out the opponent's leg by striking between the knee and the waist, usually with a kick made at an oblique angle; and a throw involves lifting an opponent off his feet and using the hip as a fulcrum to toss him onto the ground.

All of those moves—there's a huge variety of them—appear in just about every grappling martial art in one form or another. And, performed correctly, all of them will be impossible for someone with no knowledge of martial arts and no idea of what to expect to defend against.

The result for a police officer like Mark Mireles when facing a drunk troublemaker should always be that the suspect is floored, overpowered and arrested.

But these sorts of things are unlikely to work in most martial arts situations and particularly in sports competitions.

When martial artists from the same disciplines face off against each other, both are aware of what the other can do, and both know what sort of attacks they're likely to face.

They also know the defensive moves that can block those attacks.

When an attack gets through then, it's not because the attack itself is unstoppable. It's because the attack was performed with greater skill than the defense was performed.

That's really the key to good martial arts. A trained martial artist should always be able to outfight an attacker with no martial arts knowledge. His moves will be unbeatable not because there are no defenses to his attacks but because his opponent doesn't know those defenses. (A truly skilled martial artist should usually be able to deter his opponent from attacking in the first place.)

When one martial artist faces another though, he can make his moves harder to beat through practice and training. That will give him more speed and more power. It will also enable him to land his blows in exactly the right place and at the right times.

And knowing a broad variety of different moves will mean that he can fit the right strike to the right opportunity.

But if his opponent is equally skilled, he won't find that any of his moves are unbeatable.

MYTH **27**

MARTIAL ARTS TRAINING IS DANGEROUS

Martial arts is a dangerous sport. It's supposed to be dangerous. Students aren't learning how to run a hundred yards in a straight line in record time. They're learning how to injure and even kill people.

It doesn't require too much effort to imagine how sparring in any form of martial arts can result in injury if it's not done with proper care and the right amount of skill and supervision.

And that applies right across the different forms of martial arts, from the most aggressive external forms to the most peaceful internal forms. A 2005 study led by Dr. Merrilee Zetaruk of the Pediatric Sports and Dance Medicine Program of the Children's Hospital at the University of Manitoba, compared injuries across five different type of martial arts: tae kwon do, aikido, kung fu, karate and tai chi.

Each of the forms contained some risk of injury that required time away from training.

The risk was highest for tae kwon do fighters. Fifty nine percent of tae kwon do students could expect to be injured so severely that they had to stop training for a while, the study found. The next most dangerous martial arts form studied though was aikido—a form which emphasizes causing minimal damage to an opponent. Fifty one percent of students could expect to be harmed practicing aikido and their injuries were like to be to the head and neck areas, upper extremities and soft tissue. Thirty eight percent of kung fu fighters become injured, 30 percent of karatekas and, most surprisingly, even 14 percent of tai chi practitioners will have to stop improving the flow of their qi after causing themselves some damage.

And according to the study, martial arts becomes more dangerous the more you do it. Students over the age of 18 and those who trained for more than three hours a week were more likely to be injured; those with at least three years of experience were twice as likely to sustain injury than less experienced martial artists.

The conclusion, say the researchers, is that tae kwon do is more dangerous than Shotokan karate; different forms of martial arts have significantly different types and distribution of injuries— but that martial arts, on the whole, is pretty safe for young athletes, especially those at the beginner or intermediate levels.

All of which might suggest that for older and more advanced students, some forms of martial arts are very dangerous and others less so. But all forms are dangerous to one degree or another.

Much though depends on how you define "danger."

Soccer isn't a dangerous sport, but it is played with studded boots and athletes who try to take each other's legs out as they're running down the field. Soccer players attempt to hit a ball with their head at the same time that someone else is trying to kick it.

Tennis is not a contact sport but it puts athletes at risk of sprained ankles, pulled muscles and, of course, tennis elbow.

And baseball players shouldn't be at risk of injury but with balls flying around at high speed and base runners diving across the ground, there's always the chance that someone is going to be hit, hurt and injured.

Few of those injuries though would be the sort that most non-athletes would consider particularly serious. Most injuries sustained by athletes tend to be the sort of muscle strains and bruising that has little affect on day-to-day life. But they do demand that an athlete rest and allow his or her body to heal before putting it under stress again.

Those sorts of injuries are inevitable in any sport. If even tai chi practitioners can pick up injuries that force them to stop pushing hands, then hurt can happen to happen anyone.

The good news though is that because martial arts appears to be so dangerous, a huge amount of effort is put into minimizing the risks.

Few martial arts instructors will allow their students to train without the right amount of protective equipment. They also make sure that athletes are properly warmed up and as students progress, they're taught the right exercises to keep their bodies in shape to cope with the stresses and challenges of kicks, punches, stretches and falls.

The care that instructors take to ensure safety is seen in the low numbers of injuries suffered by those martial arts students with least prepared bodies and the lowest amount of martial arts knowledge.

If martial artists find that they have to take more time off to recover from injury as they progress, that's usually because they're putting more effort and power into their moves. They're practicing techniques that are more complex and which demand more from their bodies. As a result, their bodies are likely to require more time to heal in the same way that a weightlifter's body needs to recover after pushing through a weight level.

Practicing martial arts may well result in injury. Usually, those injuries will be minor. They'll be the kind to limit training rather than affect life as a whole.

The biggest danger in martial arts will always be to someone foolish enough to try to attack you.

MYTH 28

WHEN FIGHTING AN ATTACKER ARMED WITH A KNIFE, YOU CAN ALWAYS STAY SAFE AND DISARM HIM QUICKLY

For many martial artists, this is what it's really all about. An attacker rarely comes empty-handed to a fight and he's even less likely to strike a martial arts pose just before he demands that you hand over your wallet. He's going to pull out a knife, make sure you see it and frighten you so much that you do exactly what he says.

Know the right martial arts move though, and he's no threat to you at all. If you're a kung fu specialist, you'll be able high-kick his knife out of his hand and follow up with a mid kick that sends him flying into a nearby garbage bin. If you're into tae kwon do, you'll be able to get in close, paralyze his arm with a nasty twist then lay him out and hold onto him with a choke hold until the cops turn up and relieve the pressure. And if you do aikido, you can wait until he makes his move then use his momentum to guide him head-first into a wall.

Whichever form of martial arts you do, your knowledge will always be enough to keep you safe and stab-free even against the most savage, sharp-bladed attacker.

In fact, if someone does wave a knife at you, your best bet is to move in quickly, attack his knife, hand, disarm him, then take him down.

If only that were true.

Martial arts students learn all sorts of different techniques. Only a small fraction of them though have the ability to kill. Most will cause pain and some may lead to disablement—a few permanently. But there's usually plenty of time to stop between delivering the first blow and delivering a final strike that ends someone's life.

You get to judge the amount of force you feel is necessary for your situation.

Someone who holds a knife isn't interested in using an appropriate amount of force. He's not concerned about technique and he doesn't care about what might happen to you or to him in the future. He just wants you to do what he says. And if you don't do what he says, one blow from his knife could be enough to kill you. Homicide studies have found that when a victim has been killed by a knife wound, the average number of stabs or slashes he received before death was... one.

That means any mistake that you make in your martial arts move won't result in you losing a fight or being forced to submit. It could mean the end of your life. Faced with an attacker armed with a knife, martial arts stops being an art and it's certainly not a sport. It's your last chance survival technique.

That means any experience you've had sparring with a partner is going to be of limited value. Apart from the fact that your fear, adrenaline and the desperation—or drunkenness—of your attacker will make this fight feel nothing like a sparring round, his moves are likely to be different too.

According to Daren Laur, a law enforcement officer and personal protection trainer, the most common strike made by an armed attacker is a "hammer strike" delivered either straight down or diagonally. That's very different to the kinds of extended stabbing or slashing often practiced in martial arts environments and which show martial arts defenses at their best. He also found that in a training exercise, only three out of 85 police officers even saw the knife prior to contact. Only ten out of the 85 officers he trained realized they had been stabbed repeatedly and 72 of them only realized they had been grappling an armed attacker when they looked at their uniforms and saw the marks left by chalked training knives.

Even those officers who did see the knife and engaged the attacker ended up taking multiple stab wounds.

And martial arts moves often focus solely on the knife hand, forgetting that an attacker has a second hand that can also dangerous. It might not deliver the same kind of fatal blow that his knife hand offers but it can wrap around your throat preventing you from defending yourself or moving into the best position to deliver your own counterattack.

While martial arts sparring tends to begin with the knife hand extended and both sides aware of what the attacker is holding, real attacks often take place with the knife hand retracted and the blade so well hidden that the victim doesn't even see it coming.

Of course, none of this means that your martial arts knowledge won't be of any help to you when challenged by someone who may be armed with a knife. Your ability to defend yourself will depend to a large extent on the type of martial arts you've studied and on the level of your skills. But it is important to remember that fighting someone armed with a knife will be different to sparring and may well be different to anything you've experienced before. It's not something that happens too often, and while that's something to be grateful for, that also means it's not something you get to practice very much either.

Often, the best strategy when faced with a knife-wielding attacker is not to get close or to engage in combat at all but to keep your distance, use thrown weapons to keep the attacker away, or better still, talk him out of putting his knife down.

If you do have to fight him, remember it only takes one mistake to cause you permanent harm.

MYTH 29

IT'S POSSIBLE TO TRAIN WITHOUT SPARRING

The main goal of most martial artists is not to get hit. If they ever find themselves in a real fight situation, they want to be able to block their attacker's blows, get in their own counters and leave the fight as unbruised as they went into it.

When a single punch can result in broken bones, concussion and even death, that makes good sense.

What doesn't seem to make sense then is to go to a gym three times a week and put your head in front of a trained martial artist in the name of practice. When you're learning martial arts to stay safe and avoid injury, sparring must surely be top of the list of things to avoid.

In theory, it could be. Martial arts is first about technique. You have to know the moves you want to perform and you have to be able to use them accurately. You have to know how to balance properly, kick at the right height and with your toes pointing in the right direction or make the right kind of fist and deliver it at an effective speed.

It's certainly possible to do all of those things without ever putting your body in front of someone else who wants to practice the same thing. Punch bags are perfectly capable of taking blow after blow without complaint, and specialized targets make for suitable replacements for a sparring partner's head and body—especially when your partner wants to use yours for the same purpose.

Solo Training: The Martial Artist's Guide to Training Alone, written by Loren Christensen, a martial arts teacher, police officer and personal bodyguard, describes more than 325 drills, techniques and exercises that anyone can practice without having to actually hit anyone—or be hit by anyone. Ranging from front and back kicks to roundhouse punches and palm heel strikes, the book describes some of the most powerful martial arts moves available and is suitable for anyone learning karate, tae kwon do or kung fu, and who wants to do it alone.

Or rather mostly alone, because even in this book Christensen makes clear that the aim of the book isn't to replace class training but to supplement it. It's supposed to help a martial artist struggling with a technique or hoping to take his moves further than he can during class time to train by himself in his own time. Christensen explains how as an instructor, he encourages his students to continue practicing at home and he can always see the improvement when a student has followed his advice.

But sparring is still important. Even tai chi, which places little emphasis on the ability to defeat an opponent or evade blows, often requires students to practice pushing hands. While there's no risk of injury in these exercises—except perhaps to the ego—they do involve testing skills against a real opponent.

There's a good reason for that. It's only through sparring that fighters can practice timing attacks and evading blows. It's one thing to imagine what a kick or a punch should look like as it heads towards your nose; it's another thing altogether when you actually see it.

And often when you spar with a different partner and see someone else do it, the experience can be different once again. Everyone practices moves slightly differently, at varying speeds and with different amounts of force. Learning to block a move performed one way will have limited effect against an attacker whose strike is faster, lower or shallower.

The same is true for you too. You might have practiced your front kick to perfection but will you be able to perform it the same way against tall and short opponents or attackers who stand straight and people who fight leaning forward? The only way to know—and learn how to adjust—is to spar with different kinds of sparring partners.

Of course, the sparring has to be done carefully and at the right moments. Muay Thai kickboxers often go months without sparring, practicing their kicks on static targets until they're honed to near-perfection.

When they do get in the ring with a partner, they do it wearing full protective gear, including head protection, aim at more targets than the one above the neck, and pull their punches to spar lightly.

For judokas, and other grappling martial arts, long periods without sparring would be even harder. Loren Christensen's book focuses on punches and kicks because it's impossible to practice throws and grapples effectively without someone to actually throw over your hip and hold in a choke.

Clearly then the need to spar depends on the type of martial arts you're practicing. If you're practicing tai chi purely as a method of relaxation rather than as a self-defense routine, then you might even be able to skip the pushing hands and focus solely on the slow movements. Just don't expect to put up much real resistance in a fight.

If you're learning kung fu or karate, you can hone your skills alone and on static targets, but it won't prepare you fully for the feeling of fist on flesh.

And that's perhaps the best reason for sparring. While you do want to stay safe, if you really want to win in a fight, you have to be prepared to get hit—and that means knowing how it feels to get hit.

Otherwise, avoid the fight with the same enthusiasm with which you avoid sparring.

MYTH **30**

IF YOU'RE GOOD AT SPARRING, YOU'RE READY FOR FIGHTING

For most martial arts then, sparring in one form or another is an important part of honing skills, improving techniques and building up the muscles necessary to perform the moves properly. But that doesn't mean that sparring is the same as fighting. In fact, sparring has long held a difficult position in many martial arts. While teachers recognized the need to practice techniques in real time and against real opponents, they also accepted their responsibility to keep their students safe, especially when the moves that were being practiced were particularly lethal.

That created a dilemma: encourage students to practice moves as they should be used in a real fight and their dojos are going to filled with injured students; tell them to hold back to limit the damage that the students would be doing to each other, and they're going to be raising a class of students well practiced in weak attacks that could get them harmed in a real fight.

It's a problem that martial arts teachers have been running into for a long time. Kano Jogoro, the founder of judo, was originally an educator and jujitsu practitioner who believed that martial arts training should be "full-contact," allowing students to properly test their skills. Training too should take place in an environment of free movement, rather than the regimented drills that were popular at the time, so that fighters could develop in a range of different circumstances. But that would have posed too great a danger to his students.

So he developed a range of new techniques that allowed the use of full power with limitations that reduced the risk of injury. These new falls and moves required new techniques to break the falls, developing into Kotokan judo, a new martial art. To ensure that judo's "free sparring," or *randori*, wasn't dangerous to the students practicing it, practitioners had to learn how to execute the techniques without hurting their opponent.

In effect, Kano had turned a martial art created for self-defense and to harm an attacker into a sport which emphasized competiveness, self-improvement and technique. The price had been the degree to which students would be able to win real fights in which no holds would be barred rather than come out the victors in sports bouts in which the limitations and rules were clear.

Kano's success at creating a martial art in which sparring could be practiced safely was a challenge for other martial arts forms. Gichin Funakoshi, the creator of Shotokan karate believed that karate's punching and kicking techniques were too dangerous to be practiced in free-sparring. His goal for karate was "one punch, one kill; one kick, one kill." Taming moves as powerful as those to make them light contact or no contact would change the very nature of karate as a martial art. It wasn't until Funakoshi died in 1957 and his student Masatoshi Nakayama took over Shotokan karate that practitioners began facing off against each other. Nakayama had practiced judo, enjoyed its *randori* bouts and wanted to bring the same challenge to karate. His solution was a light contact style that encouraged speed and fast reflexes at the expense of power and crippling blows. A referee would stop the action when a blow landed, awarding a point to the winning fighter.

Those two sparring developments should have shown how martial arts—self-defense techniques designed to cause harm—

could be practiced against a real opponent without causing injury. They might not have been perfect but they worked as a compromise between never facing a real opponent and risking real physical damage.

But changing a martial art to reduce the risk has an effect on the form itself. A real fight ends when one fighter has been hurt so much that he can no longer continue. Because sparring partners aren't hurt, a sparring bout could continue forever, a problem that karate solved by awarding points.

For tae kwon do, this became a real problem. Sports sparring usually awards a point when a blow lands. It doesn't matter whether the attack was weak or whether the defender responded with a series of beautifully placed counterattacks. The first attack would count, the point would be award and the bout would be stopped.

But tae kwon do is meant to be a defensive form of martial arts. Practitioners are not supposed to attack but wait for the attacker to make his move, then respond. Sparring—especially when it's done as part of a sport—rewards aggression and penalizes the kind of passiveness that's at the core of many martial arts.

And if that's not worrying enough, making the moves less harmful also changes the way they're made. A sparring roundhouse kick, for example, tends to be delivered with the instep because it can be made at a greater distance. A traditional roundhouse kick however, usually strikes with the ball of the foot because these kinds of blows are more powerful. Translate a sparring roundhouse kick into a real fight then and you might be able to land the blow . . . but you won't get a point and the attacker might be able to walk straight through it.

A partial solution for both of these problems has been to develop protective gear that allows fighters to spar more realistically and with greater force, and to practice continuous sparring, allowing the fight to continue and awarding points for blocks and counterattacks as well as the first strike.

Sparring then is a compromise. No martial arts instructor has put two students together and told them to give it their all since the Coliseum laid off the last gladiator. It's a safe way to practice skills and sharpen technique, but don't believe that because you're a knockout in the sparring ring, you'll be safe on the streets. Know your limitations and the limitations in which you train.

MYTH **31**

Belts and Dans are Important Measurements of Martial Skill

People who take up martial arts do it for all sorts of reasons. They might want to develop themselves, meet physical challenges, get in touch with a traditional culture, and often even create a sense of personal harmony and balance. Much depends on the kind of martial arts they want to practice.

For some students though, the goals are much simpler. They want to be black belts.

They want take their martial arts studies as far as they can go, overcome all the challenges ahead of them and push themselves beyond their own limits.

They might also want the bragging rights that come with being able to say that they've achieved the highest level in whichever martial arts they're practicing—and they want to be able to use that fact alone to ward off attackers scared of the thought of taking on a proven martial arts expert.

That might happen. A myth can have a power all of its own and letting it be known that you're a black belt in karate, judo or tae kwon do can give you so much respect that you never have to test your skills against a real opponent.

But while earning a black belt is certainly proof that a practitioner has achieved a certain level of martial ability, it might not be an important measure of a martial artist's skill.

Belts, for example, are not traditional. A grading system using colored belts was first devised by Kano Jigoro in the late nineteenth century. That might feel like a long time ago but some martial arts have been around for thousands of years—and were able to grow and develop without using belt-based grading systems. Kano's own system, in fact, only had two colors: because students trained in kimonos, they wore either a white *obi*—the belt worn on a kimono—or a black one. It wasn't until judokas began wearing *judogi*—a special judo uniform—that different color ranks were introduced.

For Kano, an educator by training, the two colors were enough to mark out advanced students with greater abilities—and responsibilities—from newer students. (The belief, held by some, that the black color of belts was caused by experienced fighters refusing to wash them until they became dark with dirt, sweat and bloodstains is just plain wrong.)

Even today though, black might not represent the peak of a fighter's ability. Jujitsu students can expect to train for around ten years before they pick up the skills necessary to earn a black belt. For the International Brazilian Jiu Jitsu Federation, they also have to be 19 years old and spent at least a year as brown belt. But their journey doesn't end there. A jujitsu black belt has a further six degrees… and another two more in which the black is alternated with red. Finally, there are ninth and tenth degree black belts who are considered "grand masters." They get to wear solid red belts.

In practice though, there are precious few jujitsu red belts. The various degrees of black belt take five or seven years to pass through and a further ten years to reach the highest level. A jujitsu fighter who qualified as a black belt at age 19 then would be at least 67 and have trained throughout his life before he was eligible to receive jujitsu's top award.

A black belt-wearing jujitsu fighter then might well be skilful at his discipline but it's the handful of red belts you really have to watch out for.

That might not be true of other martial arts though. Karate and aikido, which both use grading systems based on Kano Jigoro's teaching methods, only use black and white belts. White belt-holders have to pass through a series of grades (or *kyu*) to qualify for a black belt. They then continue their training through various degrees (or *dan*). Their black belts then don't so much mark them out as elite martial arts experts but as students who have mastered the basics of their discipline. They still have a long way to go.

The real problem is that there is no one grading system that's both international and cross-discipline. Different national organizations have different testing requirements so it's impossible to know just how skilled a black belt-wearer might be—even in the same martial art.

It's a problem that's also led to a kind of grade inflation as McDojos, martial arts schools unaffiliated to any organization, hand out meaningless black belts to any student who trains long enough and pays the fees.

And there are also plenty of martial arts disciplines, such as silat, sambo and muay Thai, that have no belt rankings at all.

Usually, it's safe to say that a martial artist who has qualified as a black belt has achieved a certain level of martial arts knowledge. But without an objective way of judging that knowledge or a single unbiased grading system, it's impossible to know exactly how skilful they might be.

And not having a black belt doesn't mean they should be messed with either!

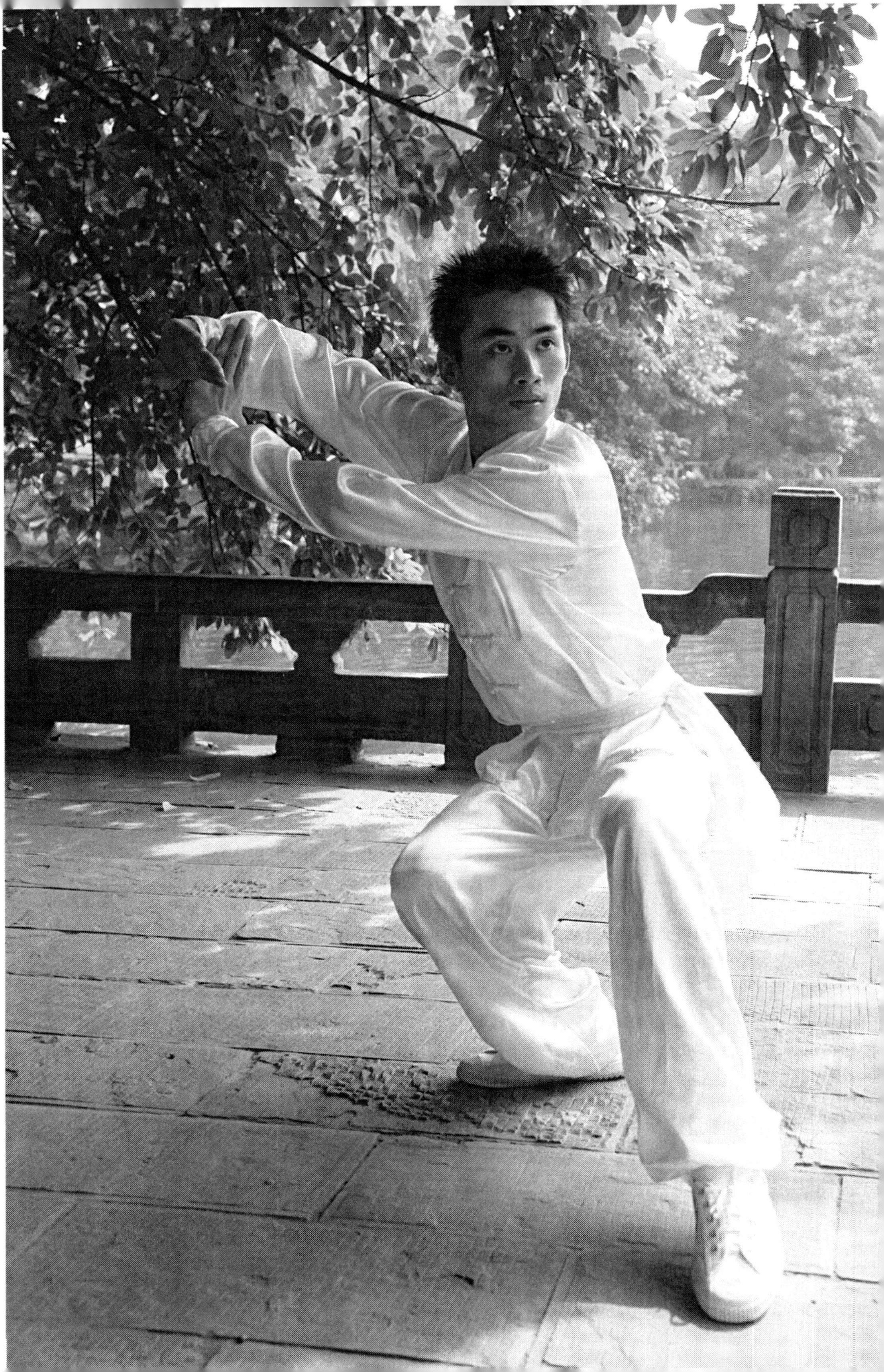

MYTH **32**

NORTHERN KUNG FU KICKS, SOUTHERN KUNG FU PUNCHES

Chinese martial arts dates back at least two thousand years. *The Spring and Autumn Annals*, a kind of official chronicle from one region of China between 722 BC and 481 BC, describes the differences between hard and soft techniques. It also says that Confucius advised the Duke of Lu to encourage the people to practice both the literary arts as well as the martial arts that were already being used to train soldiers. With such a long history, it's no surprise that over time, kung fu has developed in such different ways, creating a huge number of different schools. One count lists almost 80 different kung fu forms, including various different kinds of tai chi, xing yi quan and northern praying mantis as well as Fujian white crane and Bruce Lee's jeet kune do.

Classifying these different forms so that potential students can see the differences between them and understand what they might be learning is almost as difficult as learning the forms themselves. Kung fu forms can be categorized by "families," "sects" or "schools," for example. But those categories reveal more about how the forms were developed than their strengths and weaknesses. The five main types of tai chi were created by families who gave their own names to these forms. But those names won't tell you that the Chen family style—the oldest—uses low stances, clear silk reeling and frequent bursts of power. Nor will it tell you that the Sun style has unique footwork, open palms and high stances that make it a good exercise routine for old people.

Some critics like to talk of "The Eight Great Schools of Martial Arts," and name them after their nearest mountain. Mount Song Shaolin is just one of these, but they could just as easily have named the forms after the provinces the schools are located in, or even the cities.

More useful is the separation of kung fu schools into internal and external forms. These describe where the power in an attack comes from. For internal martial artists, power can be developed by focusing on and channeling the body's qi; for external martial artists, it means exercising to build up muscle groups. That can be helpful when the emphasis is clear. Tai chi is obviously an internal form which doesn't require a lot of physical exercise to perform well; jeet kune do, however, does stress the importance of diet and body-building. But there are few forms that don't include both elements to some degree.

The simplest way of distinguishing one set of martial arts form for another has been to divide them into northern and southern schools. Those forms that developed north of the Yangze River place an emphasis on punching; the forms that developed south of the Yangze River place an emphasis on kicking.

It's simple, it's clear. And it's mostly wrong.

That hasn't stopped people from coming up with a whole host of bizarre reasons to explain why northerners like to punch and southerners prefer to kick though.

Leun Shum and Jeanne Chin, authors of *The Secrets of Eagle Claw Kung Fu*, a description of one northern Shaolin kung fu form, claim that it's all to do with the weather. Southern China is hot and humid, they say, and martial artists often train outside wearing shorts and no shoes. Because jumping up and down on rocky ground is rough on bare feet, they learned to hit with their hands instead. The north, however, is cold and martial artists there train indoors, wearing boots. Hitting sandbags with cold hands would have been painful while kicking with padded boots would have been much easier so northerners developed a range of kicking styles.

If that sounds bizarre—and not very generous to Chinese kung fu specialists who come across as too soft to cope with cold weather and hard rocks—it's not the only strange excuse that people have come up with to give this myth a foundation. Other explanations include physique (tall northerners have longer legs, giving them an advantage what it comes to kicking); cities (southerners were more likely to fight in urban environments where close quarter punching might be more useful than long-distance kicking); rebels (southern styles are easier to learn and were developed by rebels who didn't want to spend lots of time training); and Mongolian riding styles (Mongolian invaders from the north used short stirrups which meant they could be sent flying with well-aimed jump kicks).

The fact that these explanations are so creative is a pretty good sign that there's little to this idea. In fact, if you take a close look at the martial arts forms of both north and south, you'll find plenty of punches in northern forms and lots of kicking in the south.

Ba gua zhang, for example, a northern internal form based on the eight diagrams of Taoist cosmology, has five stances and eight postures that call for pressing, pushing and penetrating hands. It contains very little in the way of kicks and much more in the way of walking, maneuvering and balance.

Wing chun, one of the most popular southern forms, has its own version of a roundhouse kick, and front kicks that strike with the heel.

Overall then, while it's tempting to believe that students of northern kung fu schools will kick and students of northern kung fu schools will punch—if only to make the differences between the schools easier to remember—don't be surprised to find that a wing chun specialist swings a leg at you, and Shaolin martial artist can deliver a hefty punch!

MYTH **33**

AIKIDO IS A "PEACEFUL" MARTIAL ART THAT REJECTS THE USE OF WEAPONS

For most martial artists, winning a fight means taking out the other guy. That doesn't have to mean landing a fatal blow, but it is likely to require a strike—or series of strikes—that at least disable an attacker enough to prevent him from continuing the fight. It's not easy to do that without hurting him, and few martial arts forms try. Most are more concerned with the welfare of the defender than the health of the attacker.

Aikido, however, is almost unique in trying to protect the attacker from injury. Created by Morihei Ueshiba, a martial arts student who became drawn towards Oomoto-kyo, a Japanese religion that developed in the late nineteenth century from Shinto, aikido attempts to deflect attackers rather than to defeat them. Practitioners learn turns and throws to use an attacker's momentum to redirect the force of the attack. In addition, throws and joint locks are used to prevent the attacker from continuing the fight.

Ueshiba has been quoted saying that the real way of a warrior is the art of peace.

It sounds like the kind of thing you're more likely to hear at a New Age love-in than a dojo in which sparring partners twist elbows and throw people on the ground.

But Ueshiba's desire to cause as little harm as possible—even while teaching a martial art—was very real. One story describes how he would scold his students for practicing their moves on trees without first covering the trunk with protective padding.

And that's where things start to get a little more complex. Aikido is a martial art, and while you can minimize the amount of damage you're trying to do to an opponent, it's just about impossible to engage in a fight without using at least some violence.

It's even impossible to train without using violence.

The first skill aikido students learn is how to fall safely—something that might be familiar to grappling martial art forms. But the sparring is a little more varied. To reduce the risk of injury, students practice set techniques rather than engage in freestyle fighting. The student who receives the technique, called an *"uke,"* initiates an attack; the practitioner, or *"nage,"* then uses an aikido move to deflect the attack and throw his attacker.

That means that in addition to learning how to fall and roll, throw and lock joints, aikido students also have to learn how to launch realistic attacks. Aikido then has a list of basic strikes that include attacks to the front of the head, the side of the head and the chest, as well as a face thrust, which is essentially a punch to the face. More advanced students also learn a battery of different kicks.

Many of the punches however are very similar to the types of moves that might have been made with a sword, and there's a good reason for that. Ueshiba had originally studied daito-ryu, a kind of jujitsu that may date back 900 years. Many of his moves are derived from that form, which incorporates a number of sword techniques.

That may explain one of the most surprising things about aikido, especially to those who consider it a form that's only interested in defense: Ueshiba's training includes weapons techniques. Those students Ueshiba criticized for harming a tree weren't attempting to deflect the tree's attack or throw the trunk onto the ground—they were hitting it with a *jo*, a kind of short staff. Other weapons used in aikido training can include spears and swords.

The idea isn't necessarily to learn how to impale an opponent or slice them into small pieces but weapons training is used as a teaching tool to develop an understanding of distance, rhythm, breathing, body manipulation, footwork, and use of the hand as a sword (or "*shutou*").

That last benefit is particularly important. In the book *Aikido*, Doshu Kisshomaru Ueshiba, Morihei Ueshiba's son and the inheritor of the aikido tradition, writes that "sword and Jyo are extension of your body and you must handle these weapons as if they have your blood running through them. Unless you can make the weapons part of your body (running blood), you have not truly trained in aikido."

In fact, one of the criticisms of aikido has been that as Ueshiba became increasingly spiritual, he emphasized the philosophical aspects of aikido at the expense of strikes to vital points and weapons training, leading to a loss of effectiveness among the form's students.

Clearly though, aikido is not a martial arts form in which you're going to learn how to use any instrument you can lay your hands on to beat off an attacker. It's not a form that's going to teach you to break limbs, snap bones or punch someone into the dust.

It will teach you how to defend yourself and to do it while bringing as little harm as possible to your opponent.

But in the process, you might just learn a few neat and simple tricks to do with sticks, punches, kicks and sharp instruments.

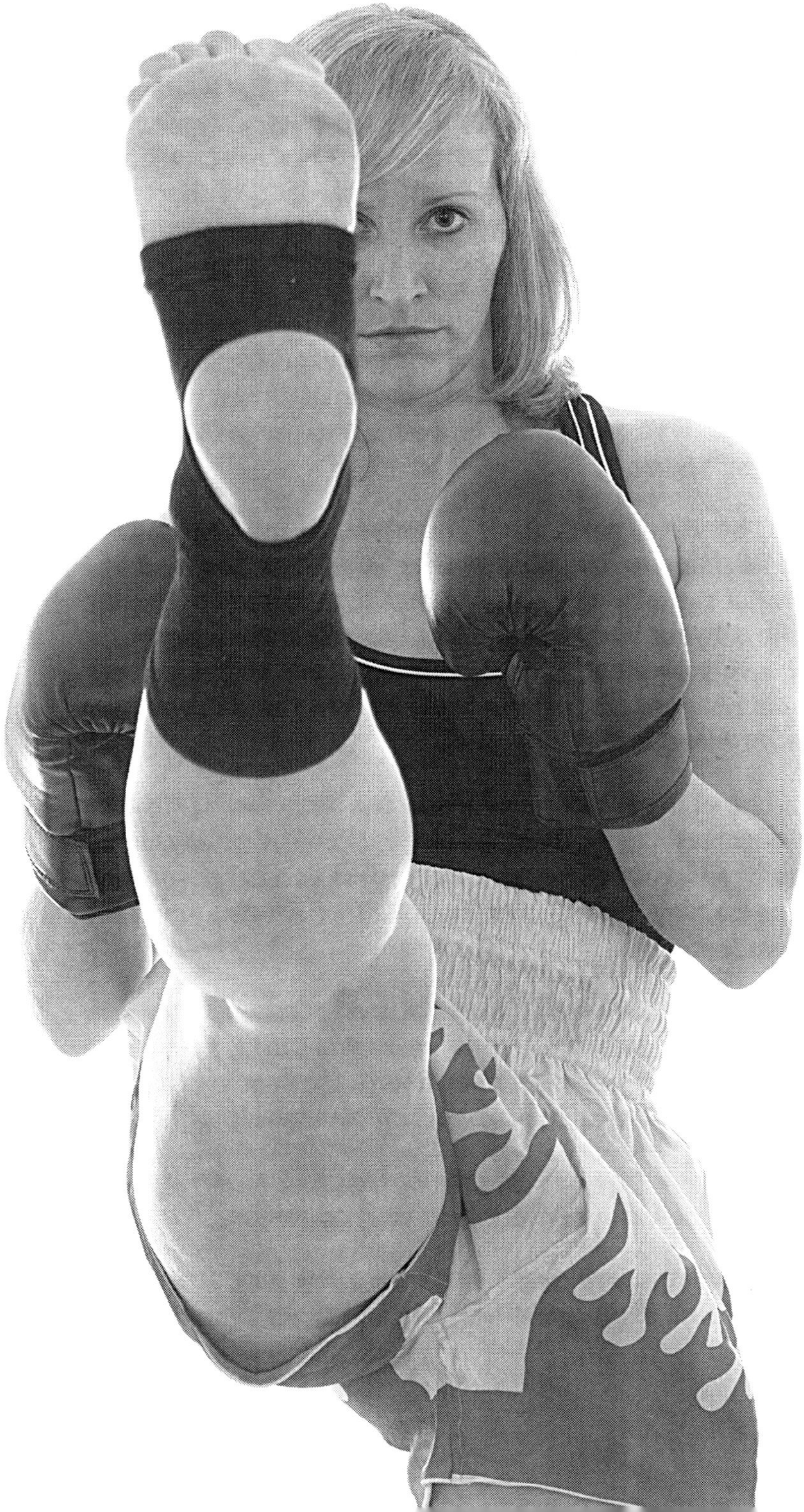

MYTH **34**

MIXED MARTIAL ARTS IS A MODERN INVENTION THAT PRIORITIZES BLOODSHED OVER SKILL

Martial arts should prepare a student for a fight, but it's not the same as fighting. The moves are limited and defined, the rules are clear and while sparring is important, it can't really be compared to the adrenaline-filled moments just before a real fight when you have no idea whether an attacker will let fly or what kind of move he might make. It's certainly rarely like the seconds it takes for that fight to develop and end.

Martial arts teaches skills, but the question that always hangs over any martial artist is how effective their knowledge would be in any real fighting situation.

It's a question that they hope they'll never have to answer but it's a safe assumption that whatever martial arts you're learning, you should always be able to beat an attacker who has no martial arts knowledge at all.

But what about an attacker who does have martial arts knowledge? How would a karateka do against a judoka? Could a wing chun fighter beat someone equally skilled in the techniques of shaolin? These are the kind of questions that martial artists have debated endlessly, comparing the strengths of one form to the weaknesses of another... and wondering what would happen if you combined the strengths of all the different martial arts forms. Surely then, you would end up with a fighting form that could beat just about anyone trained in any martial art.

You would, in effect, have created an ultimate martial arts form.

That's long been a motivating factor in martial arts, especially as different forms came into contact with each other, even in the West.

In 1887, for example, world heavyweight boxing champion John L. Sullivan stepped into the ring with his trainer William Muldoon. Muldoon, who was a former Greco-Roman wrestling champion took exactly two minutes to take Sullivan down. About a decade later, the boxing and wrestling worlds tried again. This time, Bob Fitzsimmons—who would go on to become the world's first boxing champion across three divisions—took on European Greco-Roman wrestling champion Ernest Roeber. Fitzsimmons managed to land a punch strong enough to break Roeber's cheekbone, but once Roeber had taken Fitzsimmons down, it didn't take long for an armlock to persuade the boxer to submit.

It was a pattern that was to repeat itself whenever grapplers faced off against boxers. Provided they could avoid the punches and get close, the wrestlers always had an advantage. The punches would lack power and on the ground, the wrestlers had all the moves.

Boxing versus wrestling bouts though combined two martial arts forms long practiced in Europe. It was when Europe became more familiar with Asia—and encountered Japanese and Chinese martial arts forms—that mixed martial arts really began to take off. At the beginning of the last century, a number of boxing versus jujitsu tournaments using a variety of different kinds of rules took place.

All of these kinds of competitions tested one form of martial arts against another. They weren't so much tests of skill as a test of schools. The mixed martial arts movement that emerged in the 1990s attempted to change all that.

Mixed martial arts took the two elements of a fight that had previously been tested separately—punching and kicking; and grappling—and joined them together in one martial arts form. It then turned that form into a sport so that it became possible to see who was the best fighter overall.

By setting fighters free to choose the best striking elements from all the different martial arts and then allowing them to add the best take-downs, throws, chokes and locks from the different grappling forms, a new martial arts form should emerge that was stronger than all the others.

In practice, it was found that while kickboxing was particularly useful for the striking phase of the bout, Brazilian jujitsu, a form derived from judo, brought the best results once the fighting moved to the ground.

But when fighters combined grappling with striking, continuing to punch opponents who were already on the ground, martial artists with a stronger background in forms that emphasized punching and kicking started to win more bouts... and the fighting began to look particularly nasty.

Martial arts audiences were used to seeing fights end once someone had been knocked down, or holds put into place that quickly caused a submission. The ground-and-pound phase of a martial arts bout looked about as attractive as a real pub brawl. While that made it appear realistic—with the bloodshed to match—it wasn't very artistic, and the level of violence often hides the skill involved in the fight.

Mixed martial arts then isn't new and its motivation is no different to that of any other martial arts, especially sporting forms: to turn a student into the best fighter he can be, then test those skills in a real fighting environment.

It can just look a little more brutal than most.

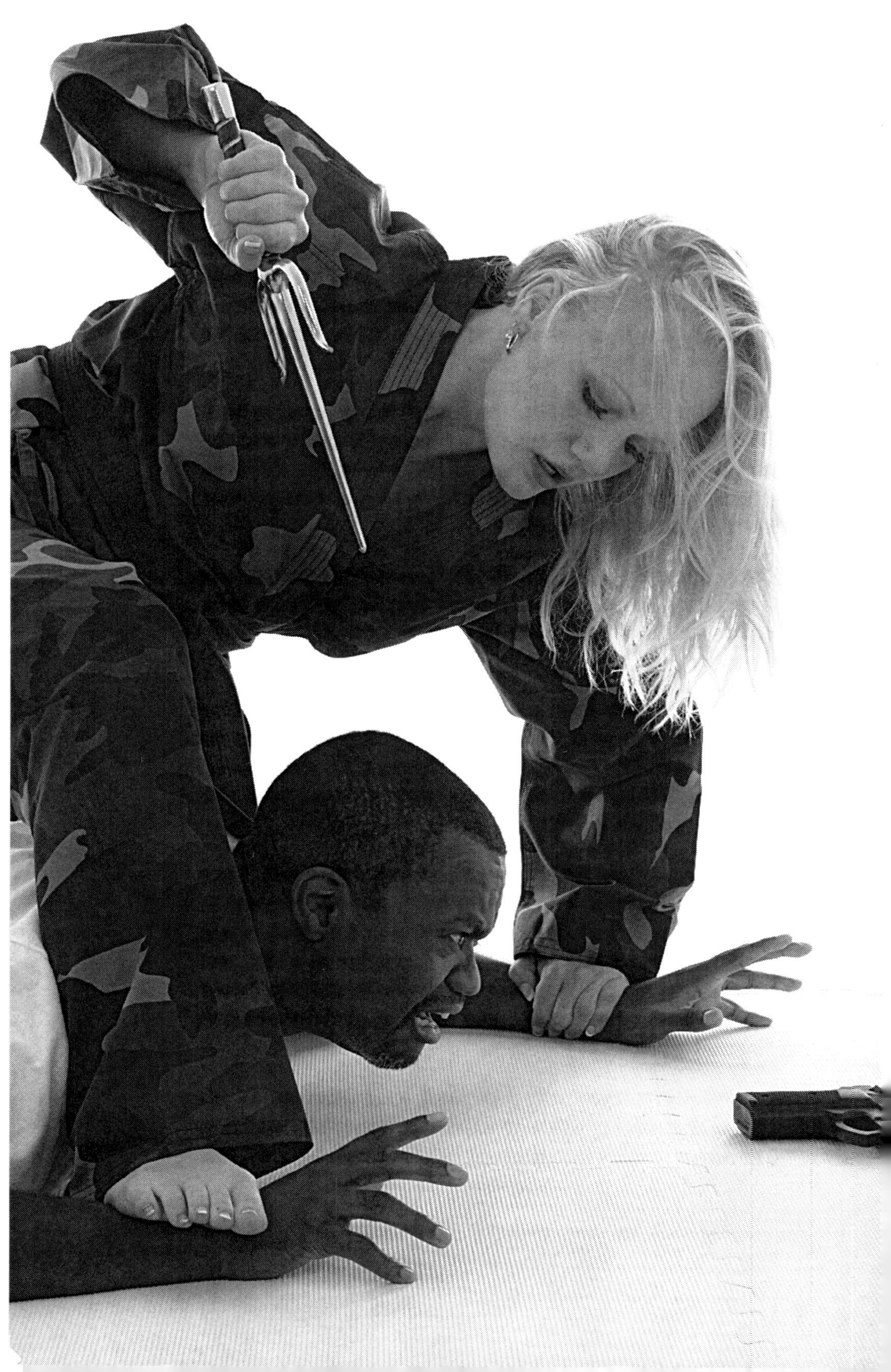

MYTH **35**

PRACTICED MARTIAL ARTISTS CAN DEFEND THEMSELVES AGAINST AN ATTACKER ARMED WITH A FIREARM

Weapons have had a huge influence on the development of martial arts. From the Shaolin temple and its experiments with staff fighting to the swords and shields of India through to the European forms and its history of jousting, duels and swordsmanship, armed combat is as vital a part of martial arts history as unarmed combat techniques.

Or it used to be until the development of the firearm.

Martial arts might be flexible and versatile but they have few answers for ranged weapons. Even the traditional schools might have explained how to handle a bandit with a sword or a soldier with a spear but you'll find very little that will help you to cope with an archer half a kilometer away. Martial arts is about close combat not fighting at a distance.

That weakness might not have mattered when ranged weapons were rare and restricted to the military. Thieves and bandits were more likely to carry a knife or a cudgel than a crossbow, and while disarming an attacker with a sharp tool was always dangerous, most martial arts forms have methods that allow them to get in close and—with care—get out alive.

Guns though have changed the picture completely. Promoted as equalizers, they only actually equalize if everyone has one and can whip it out at the same speed. For martial artists, they appear to give the attacker an unfair advantage. However fast your roundhouse kick might be, however solidly you can block a kick or apply a chokehold, you're always going to struggle to deliver your move in less time than it takes for a mugger to move his finger.

That doesn't mean it's impossible, and some martial instructors especially those who train law enforcement officers—the kind of people who need this kind of knowledge the most—do offer techniques.

Bradley J. Steiner, for example, author of *No Second Chance: Disarming the Armed Assailant*, recommends using combato to take a gun out of an attacker's hand. Now known as "defendo" combato was created at the end of World War II by Bill Underwood who based it on jujitsu. He later taught his grappling-based moves to police departments in the United States and Canada, marketing it as an "occidental system of self-protection."

Steiner understandably dismisses the idea that you should try to put your thumb between the hammer and the chamber in a cocked revolver or jam back the slide on an automatic revolver as too complex and impractical. Incredibly, that was a method that some instructors had recommended in the past. Instead he describes a range of different moves that could be used to disarm someone in a range of different situations.

If you're forced to walk forwards by someone sticking a gun in your back, for example—the kind of thing that seems to happen in movies more than in real life—you can pivot, block the gun with your arm and deliver a chop across the nose or throat of the opponent. You could then break his leg with a powerfully delivered kick.

If the attacker points a gun at your face, you can try a similar move, blocking the gun with one arm, delivering a chop with the other and following up with a technique that breaks his arm.

All of these moves though require you to be close enough to strike, something that armed assailants sensibly tend to avoid. If you have a weapon capable of killing at twenty feet, why get within an arm's length of your victim?

The real challenge for a martial artist facing an attacker armed with a firearm isn't the actual disarming—that will be dangerous but straightforward for a skilled fighter—but closing the distance before you get shot.

Other experts have recommended moving in particular ways. Against a right-handed attacker, for example, you can lead with your left foot so that you approach the opponent from the side, reaching his gun hand while avoiding his line of fire. Once you're that close, you can then employ your martial arts skills to break bones and remove his weapon.

But the books and experts that discuss these methods always point out that your chances of failure are high and the risks are enormous. They justify carrying out the moves by explaining that if there's a good chance you're going to die anyway then even a small chance of success starts to look attractive.

That's true, of course, but armed attackers rarely announce their intentions that clearly. Most people who find a gun waved in their face have to contrast the chances of being shot should they choose to attack against the chances the gunman will shoot—and face a trial for murder—if they do nothing.

If you're close enough to use your martial arts against an armed attacker, then you should find that you have the skills to defeat him—if you're prepared to try them.

If you're not within striking range though, then most martial arts will have a very limited ability to move you close enough without getting shot. Usually, you'll have to rely on a very different kind of skill: an ability to talk yourself out of a tricky situation until the cops turn up with even more guns.

MYTH **36**

TOP MARTIAL ARTISTS HAVE TO REGISTER THEIR HANDS AS WEAPONS

A black belt is usually—although not always—a good sign that you know what you're doing when it comes to close combat. It's a sign that should win you the respect of other fighters and warn off anyone who might otherwise think you're an easy target. There's only one thing that could win you bigger bragging rights: an official certificate proving that you've registered your hands as deadly weapons.

It might require a bit of bureaucratic hoop-jumping but what better proof could you offer that you're a dangerous human being than the fact the government thinks it should be keeping a close eye on you? It's like something from a spy movie, with you as the all-powerful special agent just waiting to be called into action.

And when something is this much like a spy movie, that's a pretty good sign that it only appears in the movies.

There are no special government offices whose job is to photograph hands and stamp them with a special seal. No one at the Department of Defense or even the DLV is going to ask you how much you know about your martial arts, how skilled you might be at killing people or how dangerous you are, and grade you accordingly.

Turn up at your local police station, tell them that you're a trained martial artist and that you'd like to register your hands as lethal weapons, and they'll be happy to help you: they'll think you're nuts and have you committed.

You might well be potentially the most dangerous person on the planet—without access to a nuclear weapon—but no one is going to ask you to put that on paper, and no legal authority is going to care.

Unless you actually use those hands… and that's where what looks like a very obvious myth starts to put on a bit of meat.

Although you can't register your hands as lethal weapons, the state might consider them to be lethal weapons if you use them either in self-defense or to attack someone.

In general, individuals have the right to defend themselves if attacked, and that's a right that's not affected by your martial arts knowledge. A black belt in karate is just as entitled to beat off a mugger as someone whose fighting experience consists of little more than wrestling with the wrapping on a bag of chips. What your martial arts knowledge—and what you do with your martial arts-trained hands—does affect is the amount of force you use to defeat your opponents. While laws vary from state to state and from country to country, the usual situation is that a defender is entitled to use an "appropriate" amount of force to protect himself. If someone on the subway pulls out a gun and demands money from you, you can shoot him. But if he's unarmed and merely raises a fist to you, then you're only entitled to punch him back.

The difference between a fist and a gun is clear but when an attacker is threatening with a force that's not obviously lethal, a martial artist can find himself in trouble. A prosecutor could argue that because your fist is so much more powerful than the one presented by the attacker, using your martial arts knowledge to subdue him represented unreasonable force.

Worse still, because you even know how to kill people with your hands, a prosecutor looking to pin the heaviest charge on a martial artist could argue that you should be charged not with assault but with assault "with a dangerous weapon"—your fists.

That might sound ridiculous but legally a "dangerous weapon" or a "deadly weapon" can be anything from a rifle to a shoe if it's used in the right way. A car is a tool for getting from A to B but use it to mow down a bunch of people waiting at a bus stop and it becomes a dangerous weapon.

And lawyers have actually tried to argue that fists are dangerous weapons. When boxer Scott Pemberton was arrested in 1999 for shattering someone's cheekbone during an incident of road rage, the original charge was "assault and battery with a dangerous weapon," although this was later reduce to "assault and battery." He was convicted. When boxer Michael Dokes had been charged with wife-beating a year earlier, his lawyer had been careful to point out that he hadn't used closed fists specifically to avoid a deadly weapons charge.

In practice, courts have presented different rulings on whether a fist can be classified as a dangerous weapon during legal proceedings. Some courts have declared they could be, others have rejected that position. A 1992 court case in Florida dismissed the suggestion entirely arguing that otherwise every punch could be considered assault with a deadly weapon.

But it didn't state whether the ruling applied to the hands of a martial arts whose hands have been trained as weapons.

What is clear is that while you can't register your hands as deadly weapons, it's possible that the law will regard them as weapons if you don't use them appropriately. You might know more ways of harming with your hands than your attacker does, but you don't have a free reign to do whatever you want with those hands—certified or not.

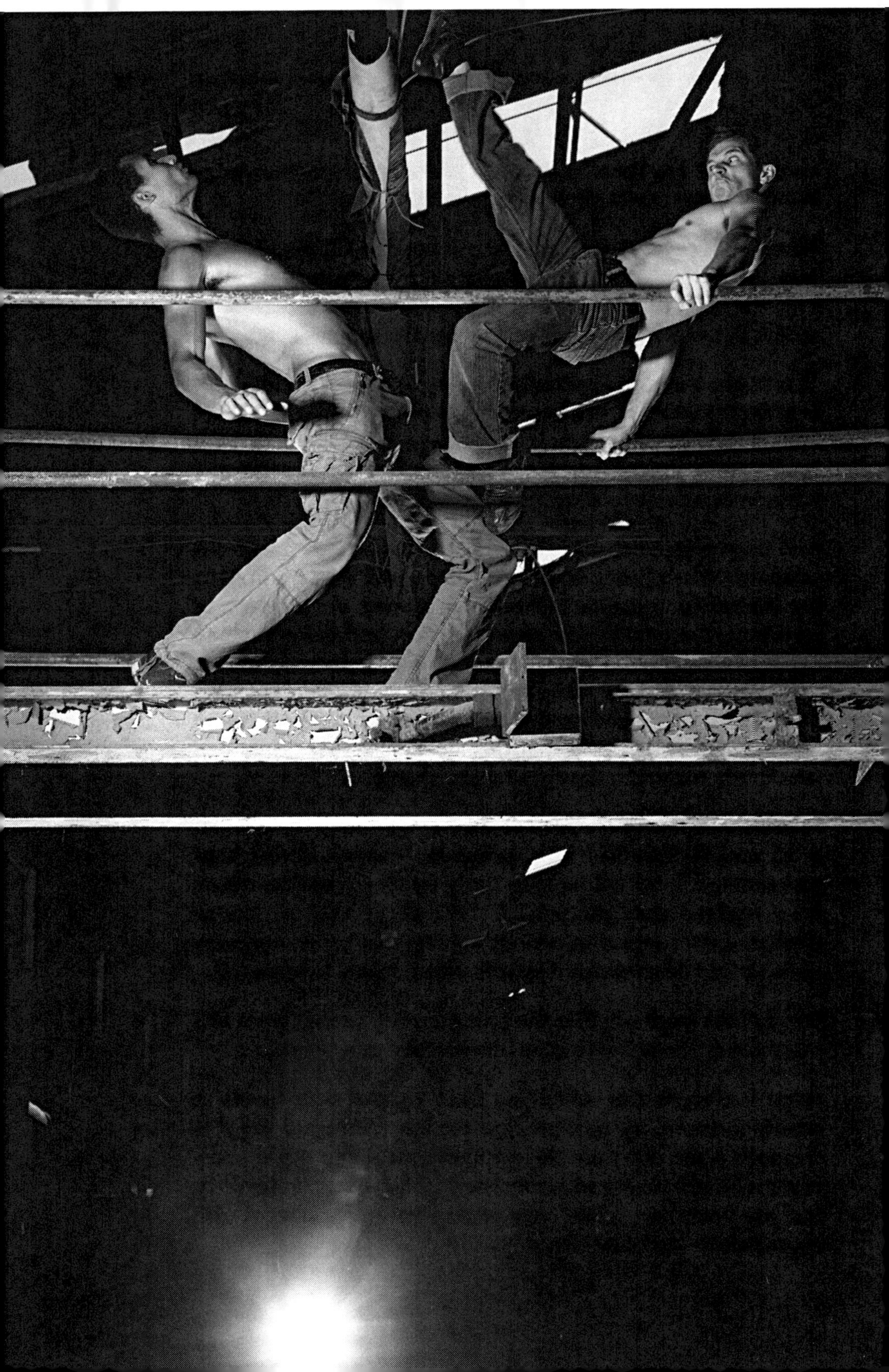

MYTH **37**

MARTIAL ARTISTS COMPETE IN SECRET DEATH MATCHES

A soldier who goes through basic training has a realistic chance of using the skills he's learnt. Depending on how long he serves and when he serves, there is always a real possibility that he'll be sent abroad and find himself on the front lines. It might not be a situation he particularly desires but at least he'll get to know for certain how good his combat skills really are.

Martial artists are rarely faced with tests like these. Most will train for years, practicing their katas, honing their skills and building up their muscles, but never laying their fist on anything more dangerous than a well-secured punch bag. It's what led to sparring and to sports bouts. With their clear rules, stoppages and point-scoring, these might not be the same as real fights but they do allow martial artists to face off against a real person—someone who moves, blocks and counter attacks.

But martial arts usually go further than basic fighting and self-defense skills. Most also teach practitioners how to kill. They assume that when someone attacks them, the fight isn't over until the cops come, your friends pull you off or the first sign of blood. It's not even over until one of you screams "uncle." It's to the death, and a martial artist who's faced with someone who knows how to kill has to know lethal techniques too.

That's something that's even harder to test for real.

But it has been done.

The Coliseum in Rome was probably the most famous venue for death matches. Armed gladiators trained in various kinds of combat fought to the end in front of large crowds. *Retiarii*, unarmored net fighters armed with a fishing net, trident and dagger, would battle one or two *secotures*, gladiators armed with short swords and small shields. A *murmillo* would take on a *thraex* and his short, curved sword. The loser died unless he had fought well enough to win the respect of the crowd and receive mercy.

But gladiator fights went out of fashion in the third century, a victim of rising Christianity—and rising costs.

There are some though who would have us believe that the gladiator tradition is in fact alive, well and thriving in secret locations, especially in the mystical Orient. There, hidden from view, in competitions known only to a handful of sifu, their top students and the criminal gangs who organize the bouts, the world's greatest fighters come together to battle to the death in a no-holds-barred contest.

It's the kind of set-up that's inspired movies like *Bloodsport* and it's a cliché that runs almost completely through martial arts literature. It's even helped some less than scrupulous martial artists attempting to turn a fast buck.

In the 1960s John Timothy Keehan, a hairdresser and karate black belt from Chicago, who had changed his name to the more exotic-sounding Count Juan Raphael Danté, claimed that he had taken part in death matches in China, killing a number of other masters. Calling himself "The Deadliest Man Alive," he marketed a manual of his dim mak, touch-of-death techniques called *World's Deadliest Fighting Secrets* in comic books. Buyers received also free membership to his Black Dragon Fighting Club.

Black Belt Magazine noted that Keehan came from a well-to-do family. He had money and he had connections. He also had ambition and a sense of entitlement that came from a lifetime of being spoilt by an overindulgent, wealthy father. It was possible, the magazine argued, that Keehan could have managed to pull strings and bribe his way into what was then a closed, Communist China. It was possible too that he would have been confident—or arrogant—enough to find and take part in death matches even at the risk of being killed himself.

But that doesn't mean he did and it doesn't mean that the death matches actually existed. The magazine also notes that the governments of both China and Thailand state that there were no death matches in their countries at that time—and there might never have been ever in their territories.

What is clear is that Keehan was a keen promoter and huckster with an eye for a buck and the kind of dramatic personality that won him fans and admirers—as well as critics and enemies. He was eventually charged with attempted arson for trying to blow up a rival dojo following a disagreement with the dojo's owner, and a battle during the so-called "Dojo War" led to the death of one of his friends. His own lawyer, mob attorney Robert Cooley, has suggested he organized a $4.3 million vault robbery in 1974.

Of course, none of this proves that there are no death matches anywhere. But then it's always impossible to prove a negative. It just suggests that Count Dante's claims to have taken part in some have to be treated with a large amount of skepticism.

There have been fights to the death in the past but there's no evidence at all that martial arts schools ever engaged in gladiatorial contests anywhere. To do so would have broken the most important spiritual lessons taught in most martial arts schools, and it's difficult to imagine that many martial artists would have been willing to risk their lives in a one-off fight—especially when, even if they lived, they wouldn't be able to tell anyone about their success.

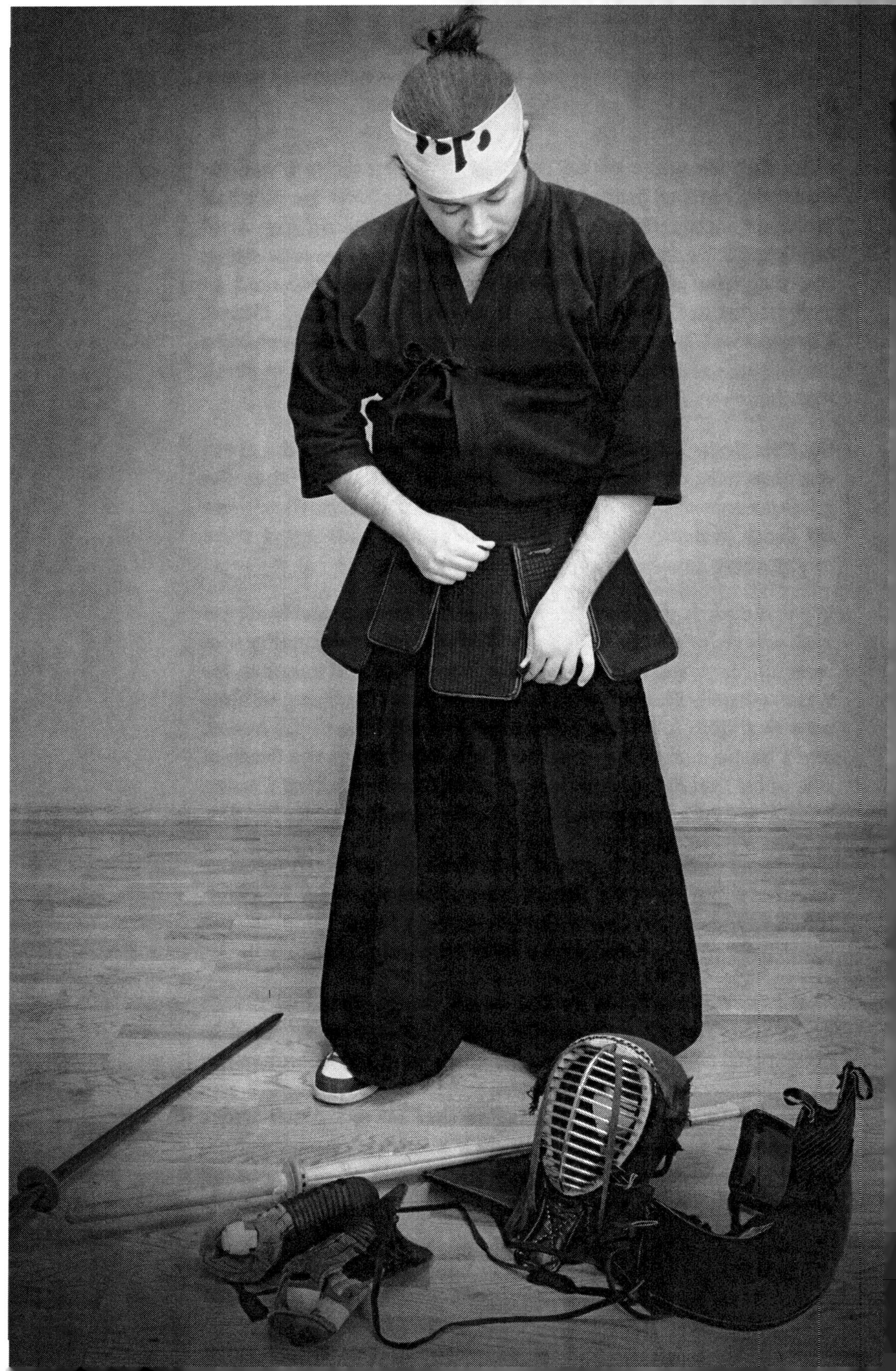

MYTH **38**

IT TAKES YEARS OF MARTIAL ARTS TRAINING BEFORE YOU'RE READY TO DEFEND YOURSELF

Martial arts students who take up aikido believing that they're about to learn a skill that will keep them safe from muggers and secure from the school bully can quickly become disappointed. Instead of spending their first class learning how to kick bad guys in the head and throw them through a wall, they spend hours learning how to fall over.

That doesn't look like self-defense. It looks like the kind of thing they've been able to do since they were two years old. They might have forgotten the skill for a while but reaching the legal drinking age soon brings back the memories. It's like falling off a bike. You don't have to wear a special uniform and attend a class to learn how to fall over.

Other grappling-style martial arts begin their classes the same way. When you're going to be spending a long time practicing moves intended to put someone else on the floor—and when other people are going to be practicing their moves on you—it's vital to understand how to how to land safely.

Being thrown though is not the most exciting thing in the world and while it might help you recover should a bully decide to push you down the hall, it's not going to make him regret his move. The same is true even for other kinds of martial art. Depending on the school, the teacher and the techniques, kung fu students can find themselves standing in line practicing the kinds of formal punches that, alone, are unlikely to be much use in a fight.

For students who take up martial arts primarily to learn how to defend themselves, it can look like they're in for a long wait—and lot of bullying—before they're able to deliver the kind of counter attack that will stop someone from messing with them.

That's not true but it's understandable that it looks that way.

The problem is that a martial arts class is not a self defense class. It's possible to learn a number of effective self defense moves in just one two-hour lesson. Colleges and community centers put on these kind of classes all the time. They don't teach martial arts but they do teach vulnerable people just enough to be able to cope should they find themselves under attack. So women learn how to deliver a knee to the groin, where to poke a finger to stop an attacker or what to do if a man grabs them by the wrist or tries to push them against a wall.

They won't learn what to do next though. Self-defense classes aren't designed to teach people how to deliver a fatal blow. They don't put them in touch with a cultural history that often includes an element of spiritualism as well as martial skills. And they certainly won't discuss honor, morality and the appropriate use of violence.

They'll aim to help someone get out of a sticky situation and give them just enough time to make a run for it.

So if someone only wants to learn how to defend themselves, and they want to pick up that knowledge as quickly as possible, then a martial arts course is probably not the best move. They'd be better off in a self defense class that *only* teaches a handful of simple but effective moves.

But that still doesn't mean that people who do want to learn martial arts—with all that means about being connected with a history, a culture, a sporting tradition and a spiritual exercise—have to study for years before they can defend themselves.

Some martial arts classes might start slowly. Others though can get right down to detail with plenty of useful moves that students could put into practice right away. Every school is different and every teacher plans his curriculum in his own way. But there are very few schools that take years to pass over knowledge that would be effective in a fight. Even courses that begin by teaching defensive moves and safe falling will soon be teaching offensive techniques and throws of their own. They may be simple, basic moves at first but they will be effective.

Or rather, they will be effective against someone who doesn't know martial arts, and that's really the point.

It takes years to become an expert at a martial art. (Sure, there are schools that will give you a black belt for doing little more than paying the registration fee. But they won't teach you martial arts. They'll just sell you a certificate.) If you're looking to become the world karate champion or win a mixed martial arts tournament then yes, you're going to have to train, practice and spar for years. Only then will you be ready to face-off against other fighters with the same degree of knowledge.

But if you're facing a mugger in an alley or a drunk in a bar, you don't need to learn how to karate chop your way through a pile of bricks or remember all of the vital strike points in the human body. You just need to know two or three moves that the average person doesn't know and can't defend against.

A little martial arts knowledge can go a very long way, especially when you're being attacked by someone with no martial arts knowledge at all. Studying martial arts—and this is true of just about any form of martial arts—should allow you to defend yourself in very little time.

It might however take you years to defend yourself effectively against another trained fighter. Fortunately, you shouldn't have to outside the sparring ring.

MYTH 39

ANYONE CAN SET THEMSELVES UP AS A MARTIAL ARTS INSTRUCTOR

This myth is, sadly, true. At least to some extent. There are no regulations that govern martial arts instructors. Teachers don't have to pass through government exams or undergo a testing program to open a martial arts school and begin accepting students.

It's perfectly possible for someone with no martial arts knowledge at all, no understanding of fitness, muscle groups and exercise, and no idea of the art they're supposed to be teaching, to call themselves a master and market themselves.

A student who walks into a community center where an instructor is offering lessons could well find himself talking to a teacher in white robes, a black belt, and the kind of confidence that's easy to believe. But for all that student knows, the instructor could have bought the black belt mail order and the confidence could come from years of practicing confidence tricks.

Except this time, the instructor won't be doing anything illegal at all.

Just as any college student can offer to tutor kids in math or history, and anyone who's ever used a hammer can ask a fee to teach home repairs, so there are no rules to prevent anyone who's seen a few Bruce Lee films to call himself a kung fu expert and invite people to come and learn his death moves.

It's a problem that's led to the rise of "McDojos," martial arts schools where the prime motivation isn't the passing on of martial arts knowledge but the accumulation of revenue by the school's owner. It's not just the quality of the teaching that's questionable in these kinds of schools. Their business practices are usually exploitative too. McDojos, for example, may offer membership of "black belt clubs"—a guarantee of a black belt in return for a commitment to train, or at least pay, for several years. No serious martial arts school would ever guarantee to award a student a black belt and no black belt would be worth anything in a school that did hand them out for money.

Other schools have used a system known as "rainbow revenue." While it's acceptable for a school to charge a testing fee when a student moves up a grade, McDojos create all sorts of sub-grades and extra belt colors, and charge more fees to move between them. The instructors might argue that these extra tests and colors help to motivate their students. But the truth is that they mostly raise more money for the teacher.

Worse still are those schools that teach a student for years and only when the time comes to prepare for the big test does the instructor inform the student that the testing fee is several thousand dollars.

And while martial arts schools may require that students buy a particular brand of protective equipment because it's the most reliable, and while some may sell that equipment themselves because they can order it in bulk, McDojos force students to buy gear exclusively from them—and charge a big mark-up.

One solution to this problem is certification. National and international martial arts federations certify instructors who have passed a set of tests and have met the right conditions. To become a tae kwon do instructor certified by the International Tae Kwon Do Association (ITA), for example, a tae kwon do martial artist must have at least a first degree black belt. He will then be able to register himself as an instructor and his school with the organization. Students can be tested through the ITA and are sent their certificates directly from the association's international headquarters to reduce the risk of fraud.

Most other martial arts disciplines operate in the same way, awarding certifications to ensure that the instructor has at least obtained a certain level of knowledge.

But even this doesn't solve all of the problems surrounding the reliability of martial arts instructors. Political in-fighting within martial arts disciplines means that the same martial art may have a number of different associations. A student assessing a martial arts school will have no idea about the different teaching requirements demanded by the different groups, and the associations themselves have an incentive to lower their requirements. Make an instructor easier to accredit, and the group will have more teachers and more students, enabling it to grow faster at the expense of other groups—and at the expense of the quality of the martial art itself.

But even if an association requires that an instructor should be a qualified black belt, not every black belt should qualify as an instructor.

Perhaps the most important restriction on the ability of anyone to set themselves up as a martial arts instructor then isn't the various associations and their accreditation requirements. And certainly isn't the law: it's the reaction of the market.

A martial arts school that's more interested in profit than in the education of its students will find it hard to bring in new people. Word will spread that the school is expensive, the teaching poor and the martial arts moves taught far from satisfying.

While anyone can set themselves up as a martial arts instructor, it takes someone passionate about martial arts, dedicated to advancing the knowledge of their martial arts form and devoted to their students to build a successful martial arts school.

That's not a requirement you'll read about in any association's guidelines but it is the most effective.

MYTH 40

MARTIAL ARTS PRACTITIONERS HAVE TO BE AT THE PEAK OF PHYSICAL FITNESS

The easiest way to disprove the myth that martial artists have to be super-fit is to watch a sumo fight. A martial art with a rich tradition, a long history and a link with Japan's national religion, Shinto, sumo's practitioners are big. The average height of a sumo wrestler is about 5' 11" and the average weight... around 400 pounds. Much of the training of a sumo wrestler involves not just practicing techniques but putting on weight. Wrestlers usually skip breakfast but settle down to a big lunch of *chankonabe*, a fish, meat and vegetable stew served with rice, which they eat with a big mug of beer. Then they have a nice little nap to make sure the food goes down nicely—and settles on their stomach. That's the kind of training that couch potatoes up and down the country do every weekend.

On the downside, sumo wrestlers also have a life expectancy ten years lower than that of the average Japanese man. The regular beer-drinking gives them liver problems, the additional stress on their joints can cause arthritis and, worse of all, they have to wrestle in what look like giant diapers. It's perhaps no wonder that sumo wrestling has failed to catch on in many places outside Japan.

Other forms of martial arts though have caught on worldwide and while originally the main motivation might have been the chance to look cool while learning combat skills, for many martial arts students today, fitness is as important a selling point as fighting. Actress Lucy Liu is said to have taken up eskrima, a Filipino martial art performed with sticks and knives, to stay in shape, while Tom Cruise and Demi Moore are reported to be keen jeet kune do fighters. Karmaa, a martial arts gym in London that teaches kickboxing, jujitsu, and Zen-do, a type of kickboxing, has a 60 percent female clientele that includes a number of celebrities. They come mostly for the workout with the self-defense a useful bonus.

It's an approach that makes sense. A strong kick is believed to require nine times more energy to produce than a punch, so a sixty-minute kickboxing session could easily burn off 600 calories, making it a useful exercise. Whether an hour of kicking would also translate into usable martial skills is more debatable. A student might learn how to deliver a heel to the chin but if they can't block, balance or put together a combination of strikes that take out an opponent, it's not certain that they'd have the confidence to fight back.

On the other hand, they might be fit enough to make a run for it.

It's clear then that even if you're not at the peak of physical fitness when you start practicing martial arts, continue training and you should be fairly fit at the end.

How fit though depends on the type of martial arts you practice and what you put into the training.

One of the criticisms that Bruce Lee brought to martial arts was that students didn't put enough effort into physical conditioning. They might practice strengthening their qi but when it came to building up their muscles, workouts often stopped at a few stretching exercises. Technique and skill was always far more important than physical development.

When he created jeet kune do then, Lee made sure that it contained all of the elements of physical fitness from cardiovascular work to strength and endurance. A student of jeet kune do then who trains carefully and pays as much attention to working out as he does to practicing his punches and kicks should find that he or she becomes both muscular and healthy.

But when most people take up martial arts, they're usually neither and that shouldn't be a problem.

Clearly, some martial arts are going to be better suited for people of different sizes. Kickboxing and tae kwon do can make good sports and fitness regimes for tall people. Their extra reach can give them an advantage that brings success, and that success can encourage them to continue, working out in the process.

Tai chi is a good exercise for overweight people. It's low impact and emphasizes flexibility and balance over speed and power. While it might not help them to lose pounds, it is something that can give them martial arts knowledge without all of the difficulties involved free sparring and high kicking.

Alternatively, a martial art that emphasizes the use of leverage and momentum, such as aikido and judo, could also be easily practiced by someone who's not at the height of physical fitness—at least when they begin.

And when it comes to the training itself, a good instructor should be able to adapt his program and exercise routine so that it's suitable for all his students, regardless of their size.

One of the advantages of martial arts is that it's open to everyone of every age and every size. You don't have to be fit to practice martial arts but the process of becoming a good fighter is likely to make you into a toned fighter too.

Just steer clear of the beer and stew.

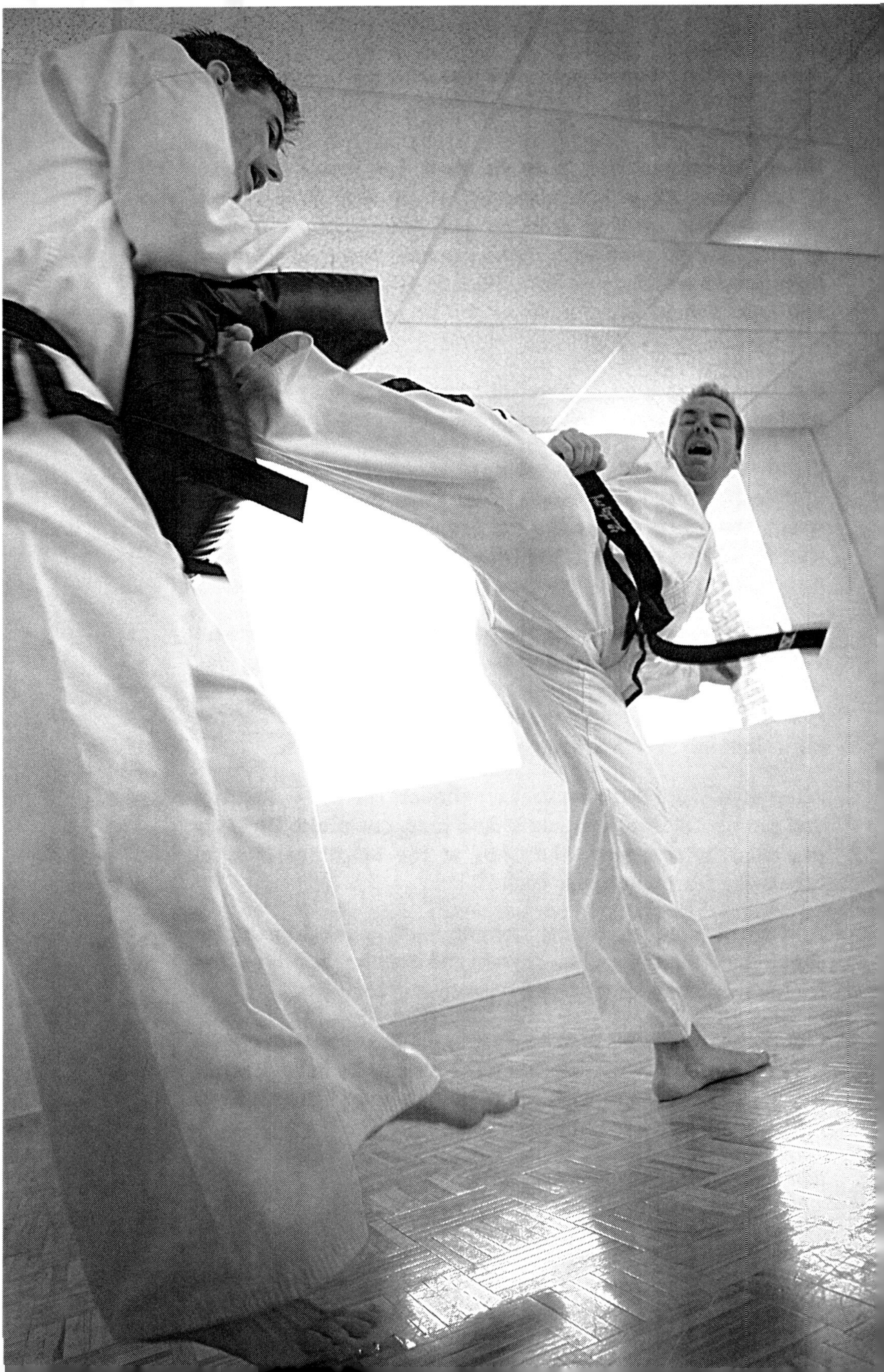

MYTH 41

STUDYING MARTIAL ARTS MEANS DOING ALL SORTS OF PAINFUL AND DIFFICULT EXERCISES

Martial arts teach students to do a huge range of things that they might not have even considered doing otherwise. Some of those things might be fairly simple, such as hitting a punch bag or kicking a target.

Others might appear to be considerably more challenging, such as dropping into a splits position or rolling over someone's hips while they hold onto your arm.

And some of them might look almost impossible, such as punching through bricks or smashing wood with your forehead.

Conditioning your body so that you can complete those sorts of moves without causing yourself some serious damage might take time. And clearly, some of them are going to hurt at least a little. Martial artists have been known to punch bags of gravel to toughen up their knuckles or smack wooden posts topped with rough rope. When you're more used to skipping rope, that alone can look pretty frightening.

But these types of exercise are relatively rare and they're also fairly straightforward. Even martial artists who practice Iron

Palm training begin by punching sand before moving onto the really rough stuff. For the most part, practitioners of external martial arts will be looking to overcome physical challenges that are very similar to the challenges faced by any athlete.

There is however another side to Eastern martial arts: an internal side.

In addition to helping fighters control their muscles, stretch their ligaments and achieve a greater flexibility, Eastern martial arts also teach students how to control their qi. Unlike physical conditioning, that does appear to leave plenty of opportunity for all sorts of strange exercises designed to control the body's energy, maintain calmness and build inner power.

Meditation is the most obvious of these. Few martial arts schools in the West devote a great deal of time to quiet contemplation but for the monks of the Shaolin temple and the other holy places where martial arts was centered in China, meditation formed a vital part of the day—and an important element in their martial arts training.

Many of those exercises, especially those practiced by students of internal martial arts, can also appear very similar to yoga. Bruce Frantzis, author of *The Power of Internal Martial Arts and Chi: Combat and Energy Secrets of Ba Gua, tai chi and Hsing-I*, has argued that while the practice of the first four stages of external yoga are often different to those used by martial artists from Taoist schools such as ba gua, tai chi and xing yi, the basic principles are the same. However, the four internal stages of yoga, he says—*pratyahara*, or sense withdrawal; *dharana*, or concentration; *dhyana*, or meditation; and *samadhi*, a kind of extreme calmness—are "parallel to the chi practices of Taoist martial arts."

One of the strangest martial arts exercises though is a routine called "Dragon Fire in Ice Storm." Intended as way of maintaining health rather than increase a martial artist's fighting ability, the exercise involves raising and lowering the body's temperature so that it rises to a fever and drops into a kind of self-induced hypothermia.

MYTH 41: STUDYING MARTIAL ARTS MEANS DOING PAINFUL AND DIFFICULT EXERCISES   **169**

It's an exercise that requires a huge amount of focus and self-control. The aim is to create the same kind of environment that the body would feel if it underwent an ice bath or a sauna. The theory is that because germs prefer stable temperatures, this method should kill off infections before they have a chance to spread, preventing the fighter from getting sick and enabling him to maintain peak physical fitness.

It's no surprise then that internal martial arts exercises would look a little odd.

It all sounds as though a fighter who joins a martial arts school in the hope of learning how to deliver a death blow to a rival could well find himself sitting in the lotus position and saying "om." He might think he's joined a yoga class, a new age meeting center or some sort of course for contractors who prefer to use their hands instead of their tools.

And he could also be putting himself through the kind of fevers and chills usually only experienced by the seriously ill.

In practice though, things rarely happen that way.

It might be true that if you take up ba gua, xing yi, tai chi or one of the other strongly internal martial arts forms, you might well find yourself spending lots of time doing meditation or practicing some very odd exercises. You'll be concentrating on yourself at least as much as keeping an eye on your opponent—assuming that you have one.

But if you take an external martial arts, especially in the West, it's likely that most of your exercises will consist of little more than gentle stretches and pulls. You might be asked to do weight training and cardiovascular work, especially as you continue with your martial art and want to put some extra power into your kicks, punches and throws. But these will look very familiar to anyone who has ever had a workout.

When you consider the range and origins of martial arts, you shouldn't be surprised to find that some forms come with some unusual exercises. But it doesn't happen often—and for those who are attracted by them, they're part of what makes martial arts so interesting.

MYTH 42

ALL MARTIAL ARTS ARE THE SAME

Bump into a mugger in an alley with a mean manner and an eye on your wallet and you've got three choices: you can hand over your hard-earned cash and hope he doesn't kill you anyway; you can run and hope he doesn't catch you; or you can stand and fight.

Choose to fight and your next set of choices gets easier. Will your first strike be a punch or a kick? After that, it's just a matter of choosing which kind of punch to deliver or where to aim your foot to cause the maximum amount of pain in the shortest amount of time.

So it really doesn't matter what kind of martial art you study. They're all the same really: punches and kicks delivered in ways that only differ slightly. And all of them are going to be effective against someone whose idea of combat skill is to pull a knife on someone who's packing nothing more dangerous than an annoying ringtone.

In fact, the differences between various kinds of martial art can be both huge and subtle. Martial arts are practiced in countries from Mongolia to Martinique, and counting them can be as difficult as pronouncing the name of Hóa Quyên Đạo, a Vietnamese martial art. Over 400 can be identified by name alone, including eskrima, a Filipino martial art, angampora, a Sri Lankan form that uses butterfly-like leaps, and gouren, a style of wrestling popular in the French region of Brittany.

But many of these forms can be divided into separate parts, while others have branched off to form new schools of martial arts in their own right. Pananjakman, for example, is the kicking element of escrima; panantukan is the boxing part. Kung fu consists of at least a hundred different forms and sub-forms, including Fujian white crane, Tibetan white crane and white dragon, Pai family method.

Sometimes the differences between the forms, and especially the variations within the forms, can be so small that the techniques can appear to be the same. To the untrained eye, all tai chi looks like kung fu practiced in slow motion. To those with a close understanding of tai chi though, Chen style is practiced in a lower stance and uses frequent burst of power. The Hao branch of Wu style places a greater emphasis on balance and internal focus. Sun style has unique footwork and few explosive power bursts.

It's not likely that someone considering learning tai chi though will set out specifically to take up one of the five styles. It's more likely that they'll choose to study the form that their local master teaches. The fact that his stances might be high or low, or that he teaches footwork in one way rather than another won't matter a great deal. As the student builds up his knowledge, he might decide that a particular branch suits him better but initially at least, these kind of subtle differences will be less important than the fact that he's learning an internal martial art that's practiced standing up and whose main aim is relaxation and health rather than aggression and self-defense.

It's at that level that the differences between martial arts are most acute and most important.

While it's possible to divide martial arts geographically, it might be more helpful to classify them according to how they're used and why they're practiced.

The biggest difference between martial arts is whether they're practiced standing up or on the ground.

Fights usually begin standing up, with two opponents facing off against each other. There's a quick flurry of punches, perhaps the odd raised knee but quickly the two fighters close the distance, grapple, fall to the floor and wrestle. In general, martial arts schools have tended to focus on just one of these fighting stages.

So kung fu will train martial artists to deliver perfectly-delivered punches and crippling kicks. But if those strikes fail to take out the opponent before he can make a grab, a kung fu fighter may find himself in trouble. That's why boxers have fared badly whenever they've fought exhibition matches against wrestlers. As long as the wrestler was capable of eating a punch, he could take the boxer to the ground where his punches lacked power. On the other hand, a judoka has to be able to get close enough to practice his moves, something that's not easy against a trained kung fu artist. Mixed martial arts gets its name not just because it combines different martial arts forms but because it combines punching and kicking with throwing and grappling—as does karate.

The difference between punching and kicking martial arts and grappling forms can be seen everywhere. The French might have wrestlers in Brittany but they also have high-kicking savate specialists who first practiced their craft in Marseille. The difference between these two kinds of martial arts—between boxing and wrestling, wing chun and judo—is perhaps the most important. It's certainly the most obvious.

Less clear to the eye is the difference between internal and external martial arts. This is a difference unique to Asian martial arts forms. Internal martial arts forms—or "soft" forms—derive their power from internal focus and the control of qi. External—or "hard" forms—rely on muscle bulk to deliver powerful blows. The result can be a martial art as spiritual as ba gua or boabom, or as aggressive as wing chun and karate. But most martial arts use qi to one degree or another.

To argue then that all martial arts are the same is to miss all of the differences—great and subtle—that distinguish them. It's like saying that beer and wine are the same because both are alcoholic drinks. It's the variety, the range and the different strengths and weaknesses of each that make martial arts so exciting.

MYTH 43

It's Enough to Learn How to Fight Standing Up

We've seen that the most significant difference between martial arts forms is whether they're practiced standing up or on the ground. Most forms focus on just one of these aspects of a fight. For muay Thai kickboxers, there's nothing that can't be achieved with a jab or a kick. For practitioners of yağlı güreş, a kind of wrestling practiced in Turkey in which participants cover themselves in olive oil, it's all about the control you can win by grabbing your opponent's leather pants and throwing him to the ground.

Students of these forms rarely feel that they're being short-changed by not knowing how to win the other half of the fight. The pleasure and satisfaction that comes from a perfectly-executed roundhouse kick, or the knowledge that they have the skills they need to defeat an opponent practicing the same set of moves, is all they need.

And often, it will be true. The kind of situations in which most martial artists believe that they'll be using their skills isn't during an attack on a rival dojo, when they'll be facing off against multiple trained attackers.

It could be in a sporting match, in which both fighters are limited by the same restrictions and neither can move the fight on to the ground. The battle isn't about who can win in a no-holds-barred scrap but who has the best martial arts skills as they're taught by that school.

Or martial artists will imagine that they'll be facing a drunk in a bar, a mugger on a subway or two guys with an eye on their girlfriend. In those situations, it won't take more than a punch or two, or a roughly-made throw, to persuade the attackers to look for a different victim.

But not all attackers are incompetent and not all fights can be won so easily.

Martial arts has become so popular now that it's likely that any attacker you meet will know at least a few simple moves. They may be enough to allow him to evade your punches or your kicks and get close enough to make them difficult to deliver.

At that point, a martial artist who has trained only in a discipline that teaches kicking and punching is almost as vulnerable as someone who has no martial arts training at all.

Sure, every martial arts teaches the importance of balance and posture. Fencers learn to bend their knees to keep their center of gravity low as they advance and retreat. Students of the "drunken" kung fu forms use constant movement to make themselves a difficult target. But all of those rules simply show how difficult it is to stay upright. The head is heavy and it doesn't take an incline of more than a few degrees to overbalance.

That's especially true when one leg is being used to deliver a kick and an opponent is running into you, shoulder-first and at high speed.

It's almost inevitable in these situations, that all of the kicking and punching skills you practiced in the gym are quickly going to look like wishful thinking. You'll wish you had spent more time learning how to fall without getting hurt.

And you'll certainly wish you knew at least a few throws and a handful of pins and chokes for when the fight does go to ground.

It's all about having a back-up. Every martial art has its strengths and weaknesses. Krav maga, for example, might be a brutal fighting system but it lacks beauty, culture and history. It's a martial art that's only interested in winning fights. Silat, on the other hand, brings with it centuries of development, attractive moves and a link to another very different fighting environment.

While loyalty to your chosen martial art is a good thing, there's also nothing wrong with learning more than one martial art.

In fact, expanding your horizons in this way can help to turn you into a better fighter overall. It was understanding the limitations of wing chun, after all, that led Bruce Lee to create jeet kune do, a flexible style that combines elements from different schools and is considered by some to be the inspiration behind mixed martial arts.

The degree to which you might need to learn more than one martial art depends on the style you're learning. For students of Brazilian jujitsu, which uses both standing and grappling techniques, or karate which despite being best known for its chops also has a number of throws, it's possible that just one will do. Tai chi students though might decide that while their main martial art teaches them calmness, balance and ways to use an opponent's momentum against him, adding a few jujitsu moves could give them some extra depth should they miss a step and allow opponent to knock them to the ground.

Whether learning a martial art that specializes in fighting on your feet is enough then depends entirely on what you're hoping to do with your knowledge. If all you want to do is practice your martial art in a competitive setting, then you won't need to know any more.

If you're hoping to use your skills in a real fight though, some knowledge of a few ground moves could help to fill in some of the gaps and add an extra layer of defense.

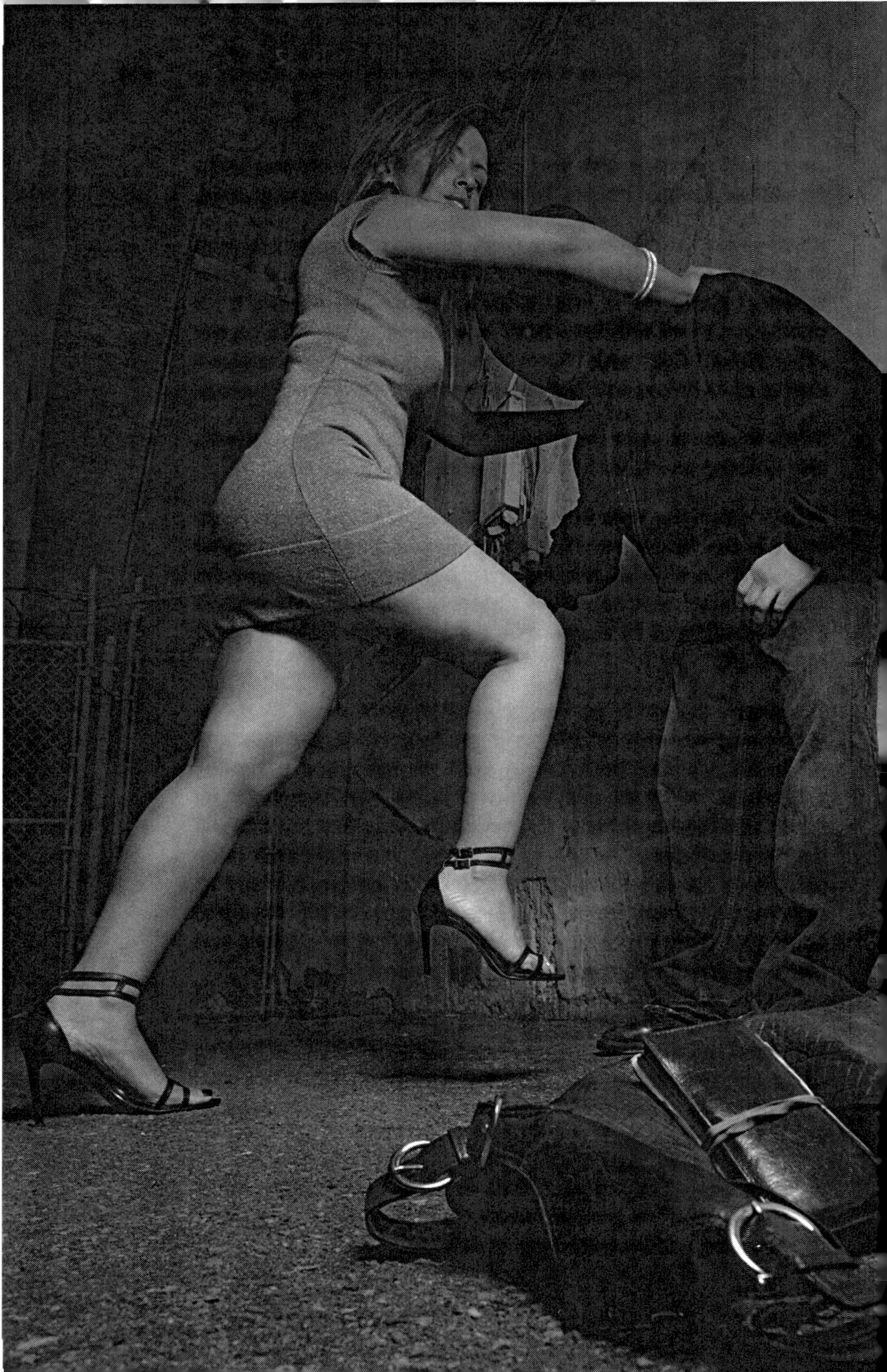

MYTH **44**

A KICK TO THE GROIN IS THE ONLY MARTIAL ARTS MOVE YOU NEED TO KNOW

Self-defense classes can contain a wide range of different techniques. Because they aren't tied to any one discipline, instructors can pick and choose the specific moves that are most likely to get the job done: that job being to disable the attacker just long enough to enable the defender to escape.

There's no room for pity or for aesthetics and none for technique. So you might learn how to stick a finger in someone's eye, deliver an elbow to the stomach of an attacker applying a chokehold from behind or snap the wrist of someone making a grab for your lapel. There's little that's pretty about these kinds of techniques but they are supposed to be effective.

There is one move though that you're just about guaranteed to learn in any self-defense class: you'll always be taught how to deliver a swift strike to the groin.

It could be delivered by a kick, by a knee or by both. If the instructor is feeling particularly cruel, he might even suggest a grab and twist.

You can see the reasoning. While most of the body's most vulnerable parts are well protected —inside the skull or behind the sternum, for example—making them difficult to reach, the testicles are an easy target.

And when they're struck, the pain is immense, effectively ending the fight with just one strongly delivered blow.

To stay safe from any attacker then—or at least any male attacker—all you have to do is practice a mid-height kick. You don't have to worry about clever throws, subtle blocks or flying punches. No practicing kata until you're doing the moves in your sleep. No punching bags until your knuckles are sore. You don't even have to work out, stretch or lift weights; even the most out of condition couch potato is capable of lifting their knee to groin-height.

One move is all it takes to take on all comers.

If only it were that easy.

The groin is just one vital point among many. It's not the easiest to hit and even a good strike isn't guaranteed to bring down an attacker.

While it's true that the groin area is relatively vulnerable, it's also easy to protect. Stances vary broadly across martial arts but almost all start at least partly side-on, with one leg placed in front of the other. That lead leg has a number of functions but one of them is to protect the groin. With a side-on stance, a straight kick only strikes the thigh or is easily blocked completely with the lower leg. To kick a martial artist in the groin then, an attacker would first have to move to his opponent's side, something that's not easy to do without giving away their intentions.

And even if the kick did manage to get through, it's possible that the effect would be minimal.

During a real fight—the only time when you're actually going to be kicking someone in the groin—adrenalin and endorphins can have a strange effect on the body's sensitivity to pain. What would be a crippling blow if it were delivered by surprise might barely be felt if it's made in the middle of a fight against someone particularly worked up.

They'll feel it the next day. They might even feel it a few minutes after the fight ends and they calm down. But in the seconds after delivering your kick, when you're hoping the attacker will be lying on the ground with his knees together, it's possible that all you'll have done is make him angry.

The real problem is that while a strike to the groin is capable of inflicting pain, it's only the pain that stops him. If he doesn't feel it, the attack has achieved nothing.

Other vital points though have a function. If struck, the result isn't just agony but at least a temporary paralysis that makes it impossible for the opponent to continue his attack. Sang H. Kim, author of *Vital Point Strikes: The Art and Science of Striking Vital Targets for Self-Defense and Combat Sports*, breaks vital points into three categories.

Lethal points are areas on the body that can result in death, usually through damage to the central nervous or cardiovascular system. Although it's very difficult to deliver enough force using just the hands rather than a sharp or blunt instrument, it is possible that a blow to the right spots on the head, neck, chest and abdomen can cause fatal hemorrhaging, shock or organ failure.

Paralyzing points can cause loss of consciousness, incapacitation or temporary paralysis. A hook or uppercut to the gallbladder, for example, can disrupt the working of the liver and cause loss of breath.

Tactical points though can make it very difficult for an opponent to continue fighting without causing him permanent or dangerous damage. A kick to the back of the knee, for example, can paralyze the tibial nerve and restrict his mobility but it won't have a long-term effect.

So with a little martial arts knowledge and an understand of the body's vital points, a defender isn't restricted to one target and she isn't reduced to hoping that she gets the opportunity to hit it. Instead, she'll have a range of different options, all of which she can use to stop her attacker and escape the fight.

MYTH 45

THERE'S NOTHING ARTISTIC ABOUT MARTIAL ARTS

Martial arts is all about hurting people. Once you strip away the strange terms, the odd training programs, and the fancy moves, all that you're left with is a system designed to teach people how to hurt, cripple or kill other people.

There's nothing uplifting or creative about martial arts. On the contrary, the violent nature of martial arts means that whichever form you want to study, martial arts will always be negative and destructive.

Sculpture and painting, literature and theater—these are artistic. They're creative, inspiring and cultural. Martial arts might be necessary but they're not artistic. We just call them "arts" to make an ugly activity sound more attractive than it really is. "Fighting skills" would be a more accurate way to describe the kinds of techniques that are taught in dojos around the world, or "combat systems."

But art? Let's leave that to paint daubers and the sculptors.

Or so critics of martial arts would have us believe. They would remove all of the cultural elements in kung fu, karate, jujitsu and all of the other fighting methods practiced across the globe so that there's nothing left but high kicks and bleeding noses.

But the cultural aspects of martial arts can't be so easily removed. They might be focused on fighting, but the differences between martial arts reveal a great deal about the countries that developed them.

Nguni stick fighting, for example, is traditional martial art practiced by Nguni herdboys in South Africa. Fighters use two long sticks: one for offense; and one for defense. Today, the fights usually take place at traditional wedding ceremonies, where fighters on the bride and groom's sides greet each other through refereed combat. The sticks themselves are a herding tool, revealing the roots of the form. Nelson Mandela is believed to have practiced stick fighting when he was young.

Usually though, the most cultural forms of martial arts tend to involve grappling. There are folk wrestling traditions that stretch from Japan's professional sumo rings to catch-as-catch-can, a traditional form practiced in the northern British county of Lancashire.

One of the most colorful types of folk wrestling (excluding luche libre, Mexico's masked professional wrestling, which is relatively new) is bökh. Practiced in Mongolia, bökh is performed at Naadam, a festival that takes place every summer. Like many types of wrestling, the idea is to force the opponent to touch the ground with a part of his body other than his feet. Unlike most kinds of wrestling though, a bout begins with the fighters dancing as they enter and leave the contest field.

Each region has its own dance. Wrestlers in Mongolia itself tend to imitate falcons or phoenixes; those from Inner Mongolia, now a region in northern China, will dance like prancing lions. In the Khülünbüir region of Inner Mongolia, they'll dance like bounding deer. All of this will be done in spectacular clothes, and it's said that the best dancers are also the best wrestlers.

Folk wrestling is usually part of an artistic event but some forms of martial arts are so aesthetic and have become so popular that they're treated as an art in themselves. That's especially true of the Chinese martial arts.

The kind of kung fu developed in Shaolin, for example, has been practiced as a performance for centuries. By turning some of the more eye-catching moves into theater, the temples were able to raise funds and continue teaching students. It's a practice that's still in use today.

The Shaolin Temple Wushu Training Center at Mount Songshan in China's Henan Province, for example, was set up with money from the National Tourism Administration and the province's local government. It has three performance teams with 100 performers who practice their moves in front of world leaders. Other troupes tour across the globe, acting as a reliable revenue stream for the schools they represent.

And their influence has been great too. Much of China's unique form of opera contains elements of martial arts—the characters regularly battle in stylized fights with sticks and swords—and of course, martial arts books have become a genre in themselves. Jin Yong, also known as Louis Cha, is the most popular martial arts author, as well as being the owner of the Hong Kong daily *Ming Pao* newspaper. Many of his fifteen stories are so long that they appear in multiple volumes. They've also been turned into more than sixty television series and movies, and dozens of role-playing video games. His martial arts books are believed to have sold more than 100 million copies.

It's clear then that martial arts can reflect the cultures they come from and they can affect the cultures they come from too. But for anyone who has ever practiced martial arts, it's clear that there is an art to performing moves well. Mongolian wrestlers might dance before and after a performance, but to a martial artist, watching two talented fighters face off and battle with carefully-timed kicks and punches or well-executed throws is as attractive and creative as any dance performance.

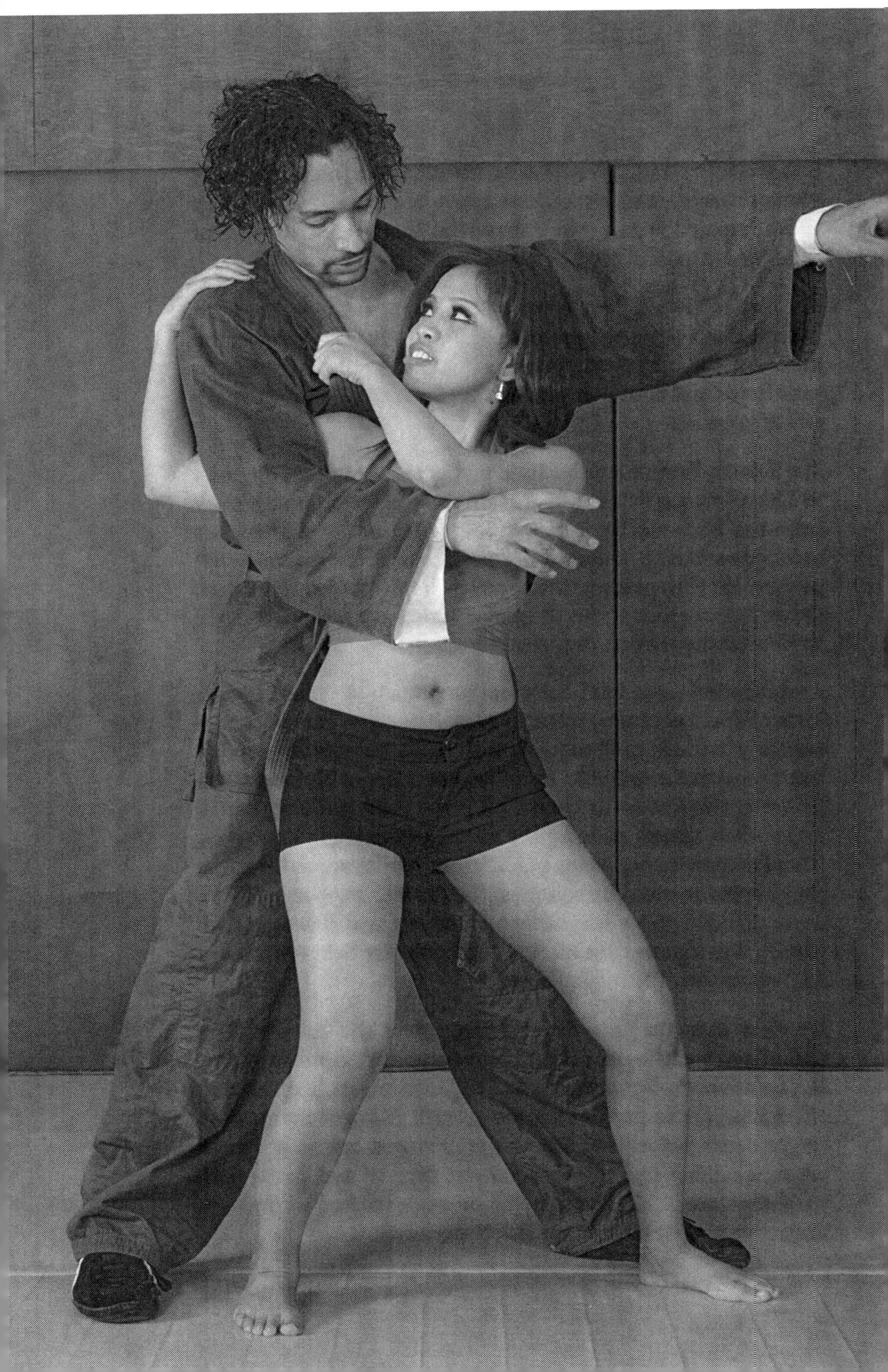

MYTH 46

MARTIAL ARTS IS THE SAME AS SELF-DEFENSE

Some martial arts myths are difficult to understand. It's hard to see why some people think women and girls shouldn't do martial arts just as a little thought quickly destroys the idea that martial artists today take part in secret death matches. But it's easy to see where the notion that martial arts is the same as self-defense comes from.

Martial arts instructors say it all the time.

The main benefit promoted in the marketing material of most martial arts school is the ability of students to protect themselves against bad guys. Study this martial arts form, the flyer says, and you'll be more confident, stronger and better able to handle yourself in a fight. If a bunch of thugs try to jump you on the way home from work, you'll be able to kick them into the middle of next week or apply a chokehold that will have them gasping for breath until the cops arrive and drag them off to jail.

All of that's true.

Any martial art worthy of the name will teach students how to defend themselves. They'll learn how to kick and punch or throw and grapple, moves that will come in useful in any fight.

But that doesn't mean that martial arts is the same as self-defense.

A self-defense course has just one goal. It aims to teach its students a handful of moves that will cause pain to an attacker.

It's possible to do that in about half an hour. It doesn't take hours to learn how to jab your finger in someone's eye or pull back a finger until it snaps. It just takes the courage—and the desperation—to actually do it when you need to.

The downside to these kinds of classes is that that they only teach a limited range of moves. Real fighting isn't just about knowing how to achieve a goal—whether that's breaking someone's leg or causing them temporary but intense pain—but knowing when to attempt it. Opportunities in combat only open for a fraction of a second. Successful fighters are able to spot them and use them before they close.

And they have the range of moves that allow them to make the most of all of those opportunities as they crop up.

Because self-defense classes only teach a few simple techniques, if the attacker doesn't present opportunities to use them, the defender could find herself struggling. It's not so easy to poke someone in the eye when they attack from behind or grab the wrists first. While martial arts have a range of different moves that can deal with a situation like that, they won't all be taught in a self-defense class.

One difference between martial arts and self-defense then is the breadth of knowledge. Martial arts will provide a much bigger toolkit of defensive moves that could be used in a fight. A self-defense class will only teach a handful of very general techniques that the teacher hopes will be usable in most combat situations.

The biggest difference though is that self-defense has just one goal, while martial arts packs a range of different benefits into its courses.

The cultural side of martial arts is clearly one of them. There's nothing cultural about self-defense; it's purely functional. But many martial arts bring with them aspects of the cultures that created them. It's impossible to practice silat, for example, without gaining some awareness of Malaysian and Southeast Asian culture.

The amount of culture that comes with a martial art varies, of course. Mixed martial arts is about as functional as self-defense. The same is true of sambo and krav maga. But forms like these are the exception. Much more common are martial arts like kung fu and capoeira which bring with them the feeling of their home countries.

And there's also the discipline that comes with a lifetime of learning.

A self-defense course can be wrapped up in an hour or two—less if you skip the practice. But martial arts takes decades to master. Working up through the ranks, changing your belt colors and adding dan levels to your grading takes years of dedication and training.

Martial arts isn't just a one-off event that gives you a few combat skills to use if you ever need them. It's a commitment. It's a promise to yourself to explore your own potential. It tells you whether you have the ability to become a better fighter than others, whether you have the focus to train even when other parts of your life are demanding your time, and whether you have the desire to grow, overcome challenges and push yourself beyond your limits.

Self-defense is a part of martial arts. It's the part that comes whether you're looking for it or not, even for students of internal forms like tai chi.

But together with those self-defense skills, martial arts brings so much more.

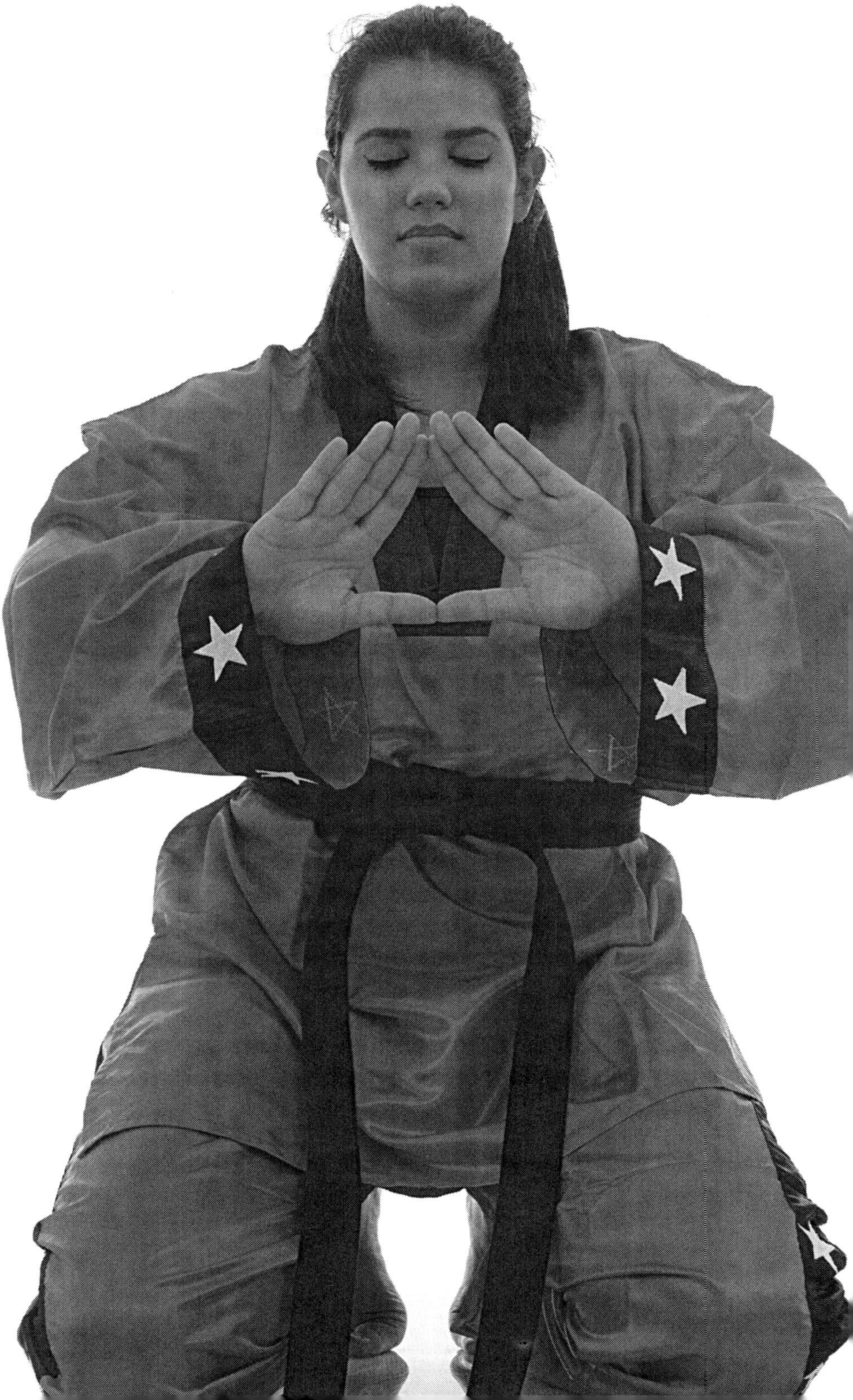

MYTH **47**

QI CAN'T REALLY TURN YOU INTO A BETTER MARTIAL ARTIST

Internal martial arts can look very strange. The moves are practiced slowly. There's little in the way of real punching and kicking, no hard workouts and a sparring routine that seems no more demanding than pushing through the subway during rush hour. Instead of beating the daylights out of punch bags or smacking targets with the balls of their feet, practitioners will be waving their arms around as though they were swatting flies in slow motion.

Sometimes, the instructor might even tell his students to stand still and close their eyes.

That's rarely a good combat tactic!

Rather than roughing up their knuckles to deliver killer punches, these students are learning how to control their qi—the internal life force which Chinese philosophy says flows through all living things.

Qi can be used for healing. Acupuncturists use needles to remove blockages on the body's meridians along which the qi is said to flow. But it's also a vital part of many Asian forms of martial arts, some of which even suggest that it's possible to strike an opponent using this internal energy alone.

For many Western martial artists however, this is nothing more than wishful thinking.

If you want to take an opponent out, they say, you have to hit them. You can't stand there with your eyes closed, projecting your "energy." Nor can you pull your punches in the hope that your qi will fly out of your body and smack into a thug running at you with a knife. That's the kind of thinking that gets you stabbed.

Qi might be fine if you want to use martial arts in some sort of New Age-y, relaxation routine but if you really want to learn how to fight, there's no point in using one of these internal forms. You have to be prepared to get your hands dirty and use brute force.

Clearly, there's nothing wrong with using the kind of brute force recommended by "external" martial arts forms. But that doesn't mean that there isn't also something to the use of qi—even if you don't believe in the existence of internal energy that flows along channels in your body.

One of the clearest and most practical uses of qi can be found in aikido, the Japanese form based on a style of jujitsu. The name itself can be translated as "the Way of unifying with life energy" and it's an internal martial art that concerns itself with the wellbeing of the attacker as well as the safety of the defender.

For practitioners of "hard" martial arts that might already seem odd. If someone has chosen to attack you, then surely they deserve whatever punishment comes their way.

Not for Morihei Ueshiba, the founder of aikido in the 1920s. He wanted to create a martial art that matched his idea of peace and reconciliation… but which still allowed the practitioner to effectively defend himself from attack. That could be achieved, he believed, by using ki—the Japanese concept of qi—to improve a defender's timing, allowing him to deflect an attack rather than absorb it.

Phong Thong Dang and Lynn Seiser, authors of *Advanced Aikido*, have described ki as having three affects on the way aikido is practiced.

First, ki influences balance. Aikido practitioners are taught to focus on the center of the body's gravity, which is also where the ki should be centered. By focusing on that point, a fighter is able to maintain a steady balance, allowing him to reorient the direction of an attack and stay vertical even as an attacker attempts to take him to the ground.

Second, understanding ki encourages relaxation. Ki, the authors argue, flows best along the body's pathways when it is unimpeded by tension. Relaxing enables the body's energy to flow freely, but it also removes tension from muscles, improving movement. That's the kind of approach recommend even in "hard" martial arts.

And thirdly, understanding ki influences movement itself. Ki, the book argues, can be thought of as flowing through the body like water, filling muscles from the bottom up and lending them support and strength. Extending the arm with the elbow pointing down and slightly bent then is both the most natural way to move and the strongest.

None of these arguments is scientific and it's possible that the reasoning behind them is just plain wrong. But even if ki doesn't exist, there's no question that balance, relaxation and careful movement can all improve the performance of a martial artist. It's possible to use the concept of qi to enhance just about any combat skill.

Qi—or ki—is used in a wide range of martial arts, and it's used in different ways. For practitioners of particularly spiritual forms of martial arts like ba gua and boabom, qi is the power that defeats an opponent.

For practitioners of aikido and wing chun, it's an element important to varying degrees that makes them into better fighters.

For any fighter though, however you think of it, qi can be used to improve balance, movement and focus.

MYTH **48**

A Trained Martial Artist Can Withstand Crippling Blows

Martial artists sometimes look like they're more than just trained fighters. They're sometimes presented as something superhuman. In martial arts films, they fly across rooftops, spin through the air like propellers, kick opponents practically into orbit... and absorb punches that we've just seen knock the plaster off a concrete building. It's as though practicing kata for a few years is enough to turn someone from an average Joe with a good left hook into a secret Clark Kent with nerves of steel and muscles of iron.

It's an idea that some aspects of martial arts itself promotes. Practitioners of some internal martial arts will swear blind that their understanding of qi means that they can blast opponents off their feet just by extending their arm and without even laying a finger on them. Or they would be able to do that once they're reached a "high enough level."

And punching through piles of bricks and thick lumps of wood certainly creates the impression that pain is for the public. Martial artists, it seems, have sensitivity that's in a whole different league, allowing them to receive blows that would take down on an ox and keep fighting even with a couple of swords sticking out of them.

Of course, there's nothing to it.

Or rather, there is something to it but not as much as many martial artists wish there was.

All martial artists are skin and bone, just like everyone else. And just like everyone else, their skin is capable of being bruised and pierced, and their bones are capable of being broken. What martial arts training can do though is help them to absorb some blows and work through the pain that other strikes deliver.

Skin, for example, can be toughened up. That's why some martial artists practice punching buckets of sand before moving up to bags of gravel. The continued effort makes the skin hard, builds calluses and can even make the bones denser. That's especially true if the conditioning is supported by a diet that allows the body to divert resources towards protecting itself against those blows.

The result should be that just as a road builder has hands that look like they can sandpaper wood while a lawyer has fingers soft enough to flick easily through his briefs, so a martial artist can develop the kinds of punching tools that are hard enough to deliver powerful blows without causing pain to the puncher.

That, at least, is the hope. In practice, tough skin, whether it's on the hands or feet, might reduce the level of pain but the thickness of the skin is only one aspect that dictates how much pain a martial artist might feel when delivering a punch or a kick. It all comes down to the amount of force delivered over the size of the area struck. A punch to the chin, for example, will be more painful to deliver than a kick to the stomach even if both the hand and foot have been conditioned. The chin is a relatively small area so the amount of resistance felt across the back of the fingers would be much higher than the force spread out across the stomach and felt on the bottom of the foot.

For the recipient though, the thickness of the skin would matter less. There isn't a great deal you can do to condition the skin on your chin. But you can condition your muscles. Working out makes the muscles stronger and larger. Because a flexed muscle is better at absorbing strikes and preventing damage from spreading through the muscle to internal organs that's particularly important.

Bruce Lee's abdominal workouts didn't just improve his mobility and movement, they also allowed him to absorb kicks and punches to his stomach that might have had a devastating effect on other fighters.

And making the muscles on your arms and legs larger improves their ability to block punches and kicks without causing damage. Most importantly, they'll protect the bone. That's vital because while there are things that martial artists can do to reduce the effect of a strike, there's little they can do once they suffer a break. Good diet can thicken bones but a good kick can also break them and even the most talented martial artist will struggle to make an impact if he's trailing a broken leg.

So thickening skin, building bone density and increasing muscle mass can all have some effect on a martial artist's ability to withstand blows. Pain thresholds count too but there's little that training can do to affect that. Some people simply have higher pain thresholds than others.

It's possible that the sort of people who stick with martial arts and continue training are also those who have particularly high thresholds. The more you train, after all, the more likely it is that you'll suffer injury at some point. Even weightlifting can hurt. If advanced martial artists look like they can withstand some painful blows then it might be because they do happen to be the sort of people that suffer less from pain.

And it could also be that the adrenalin that pumps during a fight or even a sports bout prevent them from feeling the pain during the fight itself.

To say then that martial artists can withstand crippling blows is an exaggeration. Martial artists can protect themselves a little but if a blow is "crippling" the martial artist will be crippled and unable to continue. And he'll feel it.

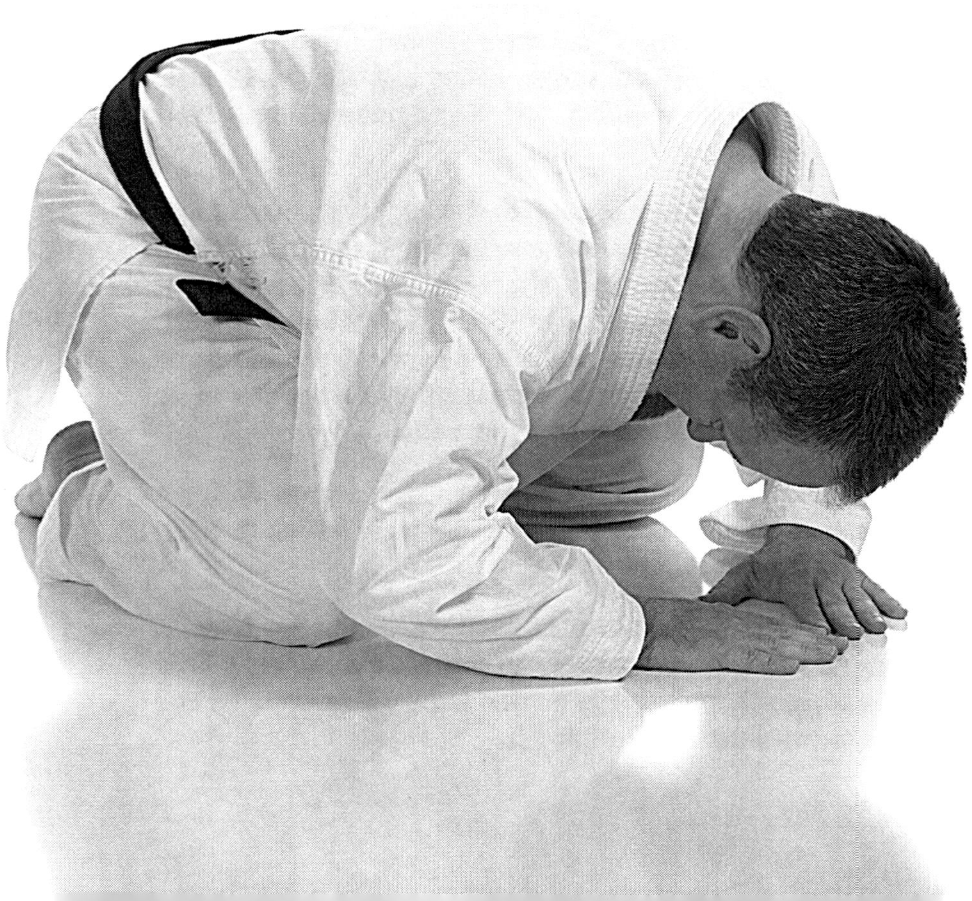

MYTH 49

MARTIAL ARTISTS HAVE TO BE SUBSERVIENT TO THEIR INSTRUCTORS

When students in the West began importing Eastern martial arts such as tae kwon do, karate and kung fu, they didn't just bring over the forms, moves and ideas. They also copied the whole dojo approach. They chose to practice in Japanese and Chinese clothes. They used the kinds of swords and staffs only previous seen in Asia. They laid down mats on the floor and stuck with the original names for the punches and kicks.

Many even took on the concept of qi, accepting it as a part of the body and a vital element in many martial arts forms.

And they also adopted the forms of address used by students towards their instructors in Japan and China.

That might have been the biggest move of all.

Most gym members are used to thinking of their personal trainer as paid help. They address them by their first name and while they're aware that they have valuable knowledge—knowledge that's at least valuable enough for them to be willing to pay for it—they regard them as equals. Or perhaps less.

Even teachers in the West are often called by their first names. The relationship is informal and while it might also be respectful, there's very little distance between even schoolchildren and the people who teach them.

In Asia though things, are very different. Students are expected to stand when the teacher walks into the room. They don't speak unless they're spoken to and they certainly don't challenge anything the teacher says.

And instead of addressing them by their first name, they use a term that denotes respect.

For Japanese martial arts, that usually means "sensei," a term that literally means "born before me." While that might suggest that it could be used to address formally anyone older, it's actually used to describe authority figures such as teachers and politicians or professionals such as doctors. It's intended to show that you acknowledge that the person you're addressing has mastered their topic, whether that's the law, medicine or even painting, poetry or art—including the martial arts.

In Chinese, the same characters that in Japanese are used to write "sensei" mean something very different: pronounced "xiansheng" the term has the same power as the English word "mister." It's a little formal but only slightly and while it might be respectful, there's no suggestion that a "xiansheng" has a higher status than the person doing the addressing.

Chinese martial arts then tend to use the term "sifu" (or "shifu" as it's pronounced in the north of the country) which means "master."

In Asia, all of this is perfectly normal and acceptable. In the West though, it can seem odd. We don't usually call our teachers "master." In fact, we don't usually call anyone "master." While we might call an older person we don't know "sir," out of respect, even bosses at work are usually called by their first names these days, and they pay us. The idea of calling someone we're *paying* "master" can seem unnecessarily subservient. It's as though the teacher, in addition to telling us to do things that hurt, is also on an ego trip and has to have his superiority acknowledged every time he's addressed.

A better way to think of the relationship between martial arts student and instructor then is to compare it to the military. In the armed forces, distance between instructors and trainees is wide. The instructors have superior rank and the trainees know not to question them. They address them as "sir" or by their rank. It's a distinction that forces trainees to pay attention and prevents them from believing they know it all and don't need to listen.

In the armed forces, that's vital. A mistake in combat can lead to death either for the trainee or for others. The distance helps to ensure that those mistakes are minimized and that the most important knowledge is transferred smoothly.

A martial arts school isn't exactly marine school. The students are civilians and the teacher is usually just someone who's studied martial arts longer than the student has. But the principle is the same. The instructor is going to be teaching moves that should protect you when you need protection most and he's going to be explaining how to cause pain to another student while assuming that you won't inflict that pain for real. It's vital that students pay attention and no less important that they don't believe that they know better and, when it comes to sparring, are free to do whatever they want.

The terms used to address martial arts instructors might seem strange but they're not meant to denote subservience. Even the bowing that takes place in some martial arts forms has no more power than a firm handshake and a look in the eye. It's how Japanese still greet each other today. Many martial arts instructors in the West don't bother with them, and even fewer will insist that students call them sensei or sifu outside the dojo.

Rather than think of these terms as a sign of subservience, think of them as a sign of respect—and a sign that you're willing to learn. That's how the instructor will see it.

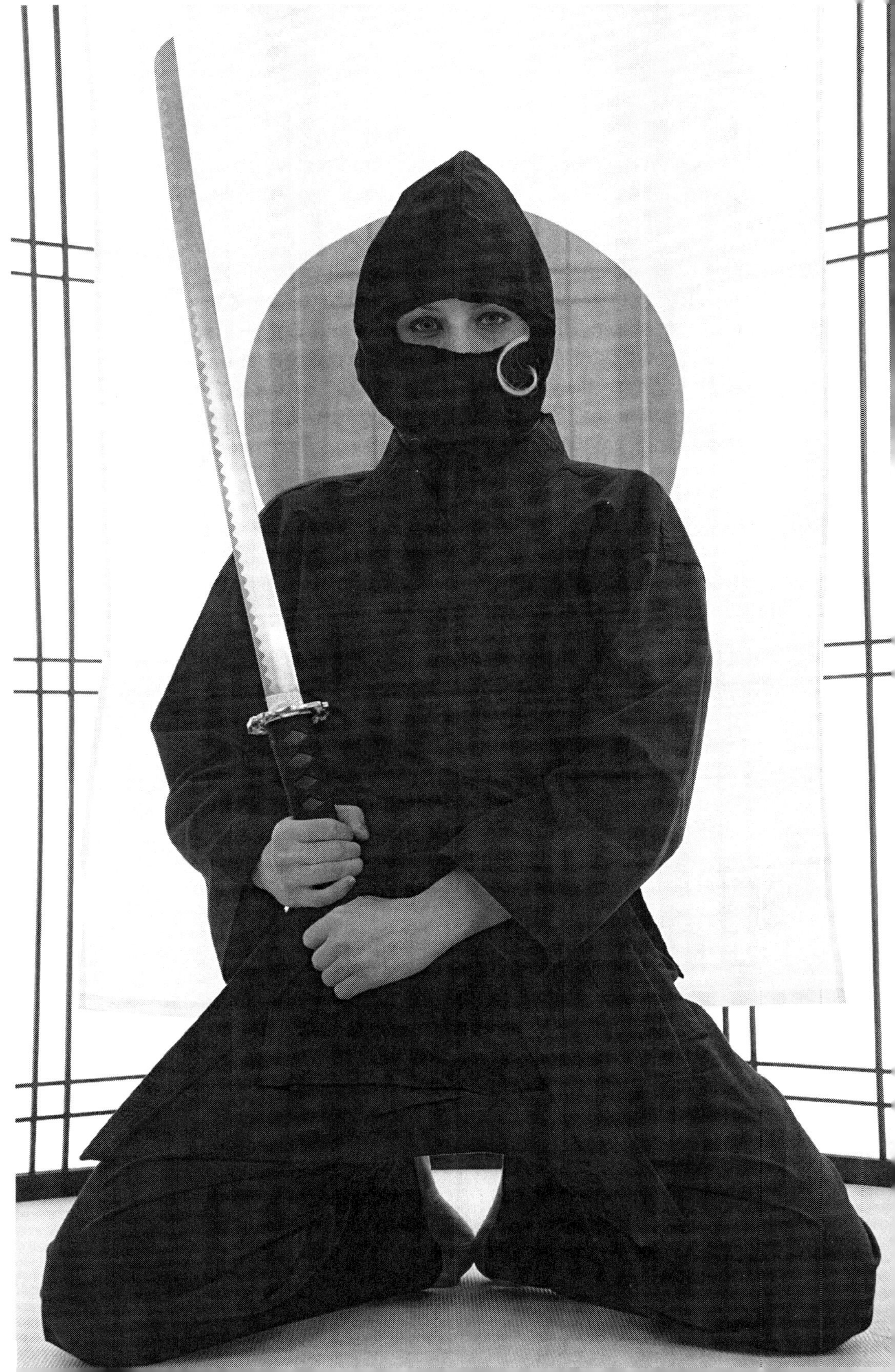

MYTH 50

A TRUE MARTIAL ARTIST WILL NEVER REVEAL HIS SECRETS

It's one of the great attractions of martial arts. Study your form long enough, develop your knowledge, build up your skills and impress enough of the most important masters, and you'll become part of a martial arts super-elite. Not only will you be able to perform all of the most advanced moves that will allow you to defeat any attacker from any discipline and do it without breaking a sweat, but—more importantly—you'll also be granted access to the innermost secrets of your school.

You'll be taught the moves that were written on ancient scrolls, hidden in a small monastery on Mount Song and passed down by word-of-mouth from instructor to the top student in each class... or each generation.

These techniques are so lethal that only a handful of martial artists have ever been taught them, and to speak of them, let alone write them in a book and sell it through adverts in martial arts magazines, is to invite instant banishment and perhaps even death at the hands of an even more accomplished martial artist.

It's the ultimate proof that you really have mastered your martial arts form and are now a leader among the world's fighters.

And unfortunately, it's total baloney.

Of course, it's impossible to say that of the hundreds of different martial arts forms practiced around the world, there are none that don't have some sort of secret moves that are only revealed to fighters who have achieved a certain level.

In fact, that's even likely. It's how education usually works. As you study, your understanding increases and you're able to do more complicated maneuvers. It's why math begins with multiplication tables and leaves the algebra until you think you've cracked the numbers game. Only then does it hit you with the kind of challenging stuff that really hurts.

It's not so much a question of hiding away secrets that aren't available to the general masses then. It's more a case of leaving the advanced material to the advanced students who are capable of handling it. Often, those are also the most dangerous moves.

But that hasn't stopped the rumors of magical, supreme information stashed away and revealed only to the discipline's superfighters.

This is particularly true of kung fu. In fact, the idea that each kung fu school has hidden secrets has become such an integral part of the form that it appears throughout Chinese martial arts literature. The stories of Jin Yong, the most popular martial arts novelist, are filled with fights in which the hero reveals the extent of his knowledge through moves that he practices against his opponents, often just before battling over a handbook of secret techniques that have been stolen from his school by a rival.

It's easy to see where these ideas came from. Internal martial arts forms in particular can make claims that are difficult to believe. Gain enough control of your qi, and you can do all sorts of bizarre things from knocking out opponents with a stare to flying through the air or catching arrows.

When it's clear that even the most talented of ba gua or xing yi practitioners aren't doing any of these things in the training room, in sparring or even in real fights, the only explanation is that these are secret methods that are only used at moments of desperate need and only known to a handful of select fighters.

It's a much better story than admitting that actually qi can help to improve balance, ease tension and increase power but it won't really have you plucking arrows out of the air or blowing away opponents with a flicked finger.

Perhaps the biggest source of these kinds of secret stories though concern the Touch of Death, or dim mak, the "top secret" techniques that allow anyone to kill another fighter simply by employing the right combination of finger moves on the right vital points on the body.

That vital points exist is well-known. That the right amount of pressure placed on some of those points can result in death is also accepted, even if it's actually quite difficult to do in unarmed practice and happens very rarely.

But the idea that you need to press your fingers in a particular combination on certain spots isn't a martial arts secret; it's a martial arts myth. It's also a story that's enabled hucksters like Count Dante to try to make a ton of cash claiming that he knows the secrets and he's prepared to reveal them in return for $9.95 including postage and package.

There are certainly things that you don't know about the martial arts that you're studying. Unless you're prepared to stick with it for the rest of your life, it's likely that there will always be things that you don't know about it.

But in general, there are no hidden secrets in martial arts. There are only techniques that you haven't yet learned and moves you're not yet ready to practice.

You don't have to be one of the super-elite for them to be revealed to you though. You just have to dedicate yourself to learning.

CONCLUSION

Martial arts have picked up a bunch of different stories over the years. Some of those stories, like those that surround the monks of the Shaolin temple, have only added to the appeal of martial arts, making students feel part of a centuries-old tradition. Others however, like the idea that martial arts is only for men or that training is all about beating people up, have had the effect of putting off good students and attracting the wrong types to martial arts schools.

This book has tried to remove many of the biggest myths that have attached themselves to martial arts to reveal what the discipline is really about.

Martial arts is more than a method of self-defense. It's a way to know yourself. It's a tool that will allow you to protect yourself when you need to. It's a discipline that will give you the ability think quickly, concentrate fully and make decisions carefully. And it's a tradition that will make you part of a community and a link in a history that stretches back thousands of years.

Martial arts might have generated dozens of bizarre stories but whichever form you choose to learn, it will have a story of its own—and as you learn and develop, you become part of that discipline's story too.

Martial arts might have created plenty of legends, but its power and the strength are no myth.

ABOUT THE AUTHOR

Sulaiman Sharif is the expert to whom the world's leading martial arts teachers turn when they want guidance. A teacher's instructor, Cikgu Sulaiman is Harimau Pelangi Cula Sakti—**Highest ranking Black belt**—and holds the rank of Black Warrior in the **Malay Warrior Art** of Silat Seni Gayong. Personally selected by Silat Gayong's founder, the late Dato' Meor Abdul Rahman, to propagate the system around the world, Cikgu Sulaiman spent seven years living and teaching martial arts instructors in Europe and a further thirteen years in the U.S. where he founded Gayong Amerika USA. After returning to Malaysia, he established Gayong International USA, which he continues to lead today. His 45 years of experience in the martial arts have allowed him to teach Silat Seni Gayong to martial artists from dozens of disciplines including krav maga, kung fu, tae kwon do and karate. His students are the masters of their martial arts forms who pass Cikgu Sulaiman's teachings to their own students.

INDEX

Acupuncture 36, 100
Age 16, 55, 56, 72, 75, 76, 128
Aikido 19, 100, 111, 112, 115, 129, 135, 136, 137, 155, 165, 192, 193, 194
Archery 32, 92
Ayurvedic medicine 100
Ba gua 12, 15, 99, 133, 168, 169, 174, 193, 204
Bak mei 51, 61
Bkyukl bökh 31, 184
Black belt 24, 72, 127, 128, 129, 147, 148, 152, 153, 157, 159, 160, 161
Boxing 7, 20, 22, 37, 41, 53, 56, 140, 172, 173
Bruce Lee 24, 43, 46, 56, 57, 61, 74, 80, 88, 89, 131, 160, 164, 177, 197
Buddhism 12, 36
Capoeira 27, 189
Chuck Norris 57
Count Danté 152, 153, 205
Da Mo 36
Dans 33, 87, 127, 129, 189
Dit da jow 104
Duels 21, 143
Evala 59
Fedor Emilianenko 55, 57
Fencing 20, 22, 49, 68, 92
Five step quan 12
Gichin Funakoshi 16, 124
Gatka 31
Gong fu 60
Gymkata 27, 28
Hard forms 7, 131, 174, 192, 193
Henan province 4, 5, 10, 185
Hironori Ohtsuka 16
Injury 21, 36, 85, 111–114, 119, 120, 123–125, 135, 136, 197
Iron Palm 103, 104, 167
Jeet kune do 24, 57, 80, 131, 132, 164, 165, 177
Jigoro Kano 15, 16, 52, 80, 123, 124, 128, 129
Johannes Liechtenauer 20
Judo 15, 16, 17, 23, 39, 41, 52, 53, 55, 59, 61, 62, 69, 72, 80, 84, 101, 123, 124, 127, 141, 165
Jujitsu 15, 16, 53, 123, 128, 129, 136, 140, 141, 144, 164, 177, 183, 192
Kalarippayattu 37, 48, 49, 68, 100
Karate 15–17, 19, 23, 29, 41, 53, 57, 61, 62, 84, 100, 111, 112, 120, 121, 124, 125, 127, 129, 148, 152, 157, 173, 174, 177, 183, 199
Kendo 9, 16, 92
Ki 192, 193
Kickboxing 21, 37, 53, 141, 164, 165
Krav maga 15, 24, 37, 69, 177, 189
Kung fu 4, 5, 11, 12, 15, 19, 23, 36, 37, 48, 51–53, 56, 59–61, 64, 68, 72, 74, 81, 91, 97, 101, 103, 105, 111, 112, 115, 120, 121, 131–133, 156, 160, 171–173, 176, 183, 185, 189, 199, 204
Kurt Thomas 27
Kwai Chang Caine 5
Luohan quan 12
McDojos 129, 160
Meridians 36, 101, 191
Mixed martial arts 7, 15, 24, 37, 52, 53, 55, 56, 88, 139–141, 157, 173, 177, 189
Morihei Ueshiba 135–137, 192
Muay thai 53, 56, 121, 129, 175
Nanchaku 91, 92
Nguni stick fighting 184
Oomoto-kyo 135
Olympics 7, 16
Silat 49, 101, 129, 177, 189
Pushing hands 65, 79, 80, 93, 113, 120
Qi 24, 36–38, 43, 44, 53, 64, 73, 77, 99–102, 104, 116, 132, 164, 168, 174, 191–195, 199, 204, 205
Qi gong 12, 37, 38, 100, 101, 104

Red belt 128, 129
Sambo 55, 69, 72, 88, 97, 129, 189
Samurai 15, 91
Self-defense 20, 24, 25, 34, 36, 37, 44, 45, 49, 52, 55, 64, 65, 69, 70, 76, 77, 80, 84, 85, 89, 121, 124, 148, 151, 155, 156, 164, 172, 179, 181, 187–189
Seven star quan lian 12
Shaolin 4, 5, 7–15, 20, 36, 37, 48, 60, 64, 68, 72, 76, 92, 132, 134, 138, 142, 168, 184, 185
Shaster vidiya 31
Shinto 135, 163
soft forms 7, 48, 131, 174
Sparring 25, 34, 40, 42, 44, 45, 59, 63, 65, 75, 79, 84, 89, 92, 93, 96, 111, 116, 117, 119–126, 136, 139, 151, 158, 165, 191, 201, 205
Staff fighting 7–9, 20, 48, 49, 65, 68, 92, 137, 143, 199
Sumo 163, 184
Tae kwon do 27, 39–41, 44, 51, 52, 61, 62, 69, 72, 73, 80, 84, 92, 93, 101, 108, 111, 112, 115, 120, 125, 127, 161, 165, 199
Tai chi (taijiquan) 12, 37–39, 60, 63–66, 71–73, 77, 79, 80, 85, 88, 99, 101, 111–113, 116, 120, 121, 131, 132, 165, 168, 169, 172, 177, 189
Taoism 12
Tianyuan 8, 9
Trial by combat 21
Wing chun 51, 56, 57, 60, 80, 133, 134, 139, 173, 174, 177, 194
Wing Chun 73, 74
Wrestling 7, 20, 22, 31, 37, 53, 55, 59, 69, 70, 80, 140, 148, 163, 172, 173, 175, 184, 185
Wushu 48, 60, 185
Xing yi 12, 131, 168, 169, 204